Fetal/Fatal Knowledge

New Reproductive Technologies and
Family-Building Strategies in India

Fetal/Fatal Knowledge

New Reproductive Technologies and Family-Building Strategies in India

SUNIL K. KHANNA

Oregon State University

 CASE STUDIES ON CONTEMPORARY SOCIAL ISSUES:
JOHN A. YOUNG, SERIES EDITOR

 **WADSWORTH**
CENGAGE Learning

Australia • Brazil • Japan • Korea • Mexico • Singapore • Spain • United Kingdom • United States

WADSWORTH
CENGAGE Learning™

Fetal/Fatal Knowledge:
New Reproductive Technologies and Family-Building Strategies in India
Sunil K. Khanna

Executive Editor: Marcus Boggs

Assistant Editor: Liana Monari

Editorial Assistant: Arwen Petty

Media Editor: Andrew Keay

Marketing Manager: Kim Russell

Marketing Assistant: Dimitri Hagnere

Marketing Communications Manager: Tami Strang

Project Manager, Editorial Production: Beth Kluckhohn

Creative Director: Rob Hugel

Print Buyer: Linda Hsu

Permissions Editor: Mardell Glinski Schultz

Production Service: Pre-PressPMG

Cover Designer: Carole Lawson

Cover Image: Sunil K. Khanna

Compositor: Pre-PressPMG

For product information and technology assistance, contact us at **Cengage Learning Academic Resource Center, 1-800-423-0563**

For permission to use material from this text or product, submit all requests online at **www.cengage.com/permissions**
Further permissions questions can be e-mailed to **permissionrequest@cengage.com**

Library of Congress Control Number: 2008941420

ISBN-13: 978-0-495-09525-5

ISBN-10: 0-495-09525-7

Wadsworth/Cengage Learning
10 Davis Drive
Belmont, CA 94002-3098
USA

Cengage Learning products are represented in Canada by Nelson Education, Ltd.

For your course and learning solutions, visit **academic.cengage.com**

Purchase any of our products at your local college store or at our preferred online store **www.ichapters.com**

Printed in Canada
1 2 3 4 5 6 7 12 11 10 09

✳

Contents

✳

Foreword

ABOUT THE SERIES

This series explores the practical applications of anthropology in understanding and addressing problems faced by human societies around the world. Each case study examines an issue of socially recognized importance in the historical, geographical, and cultural context of a particular region of the world, while adding comparative analysis to highlight not only the local effects of globalization but also the global dimensions of the issue. The authors write with a readable narrative style and include reference to their own participation, roles, and responsibilities in the communities they study. Their engagement with people goes beyond observation and research, as they explain and sometimes illustrate from personal experience how their work has implications for advocacy, community action, and policy formation. They demonstrate how anthropological investigations can build our knowledge of human societies and at the same time provide the basis for fostering community empowerment, resolving conflicts, and pursuing social justice.

ABOUT THE AUTHOR

Sunil K. Khanna is Associate Professor of Anthropology at Oregon State University. He received a PhD in Physical Anthropology from the University of Delhi, India in 1988 and a PhD in Cultural Anthropology from Syracuse University in 1995. He has been at Oregon State University since 1995. He has conducted research in India and the United States and is the author of numerous research articles and reports in the areas of family-building strategies, son preference, female-selective abortion, minority health, and cultural competency in health care.

ABOUT THIS CASE STUDY
John A. Young, Series Editor

This case study immerses the reader in the social life of an urbanizing peasant community, its members caught in a struggle to maintain their identity and family traditions as they react simultaneously to new economic opportunities and perceived social threats. India is well-known for having a male-centered family system with a strong preference for giving birth to sons, a widely shared value implicated in a skewed sex ratio favoring males in the overall population. In an intimate and revealing ethnographic study, the author reflects on his role during fieldwork as a "native" anthropologist; examines the historical and cultural underpinnings of son preference and why it persists in a community exposed to wider forces of globalization; documents the availability and use of new reproductive technologies and abortion services; and explores the cultural, ethical, and legal meanings attached to family-building strategies involving prenatal sex identification and female-selective abortion. Discussion of these practices holistically includes the voices of medical professionals, village leaders, the wealthy, the poor, and women of all ages. You will learn about the childbearing experiences of women, the family and community pressures placed on them, their interactions with doctors, and how they manage difficult choices made possible by the availability of new reproductive technologies. The author explains patriarchy in a cross-cultural context, its influence under conditions of reduced birth rates, and why government policies and regulations have not been successful in curbing female feticide. Knowledge gained from this study and the author's own advocacy establish a broader mandate for change, thus providing a foundation for effective community based interventions aimed at improving the status of women and girls.

✳

Preface

This book is about son preference and female-selective abortion in a rural peasant community experiencing urbanization, rapid economic transformation, and social change. The information is presented from a perspective informed by anthropology—a perspective that advocates for a holistic understanding of cultures that is historically informed and cognizant of the local realities. By using a case study approach, the book examines the intricate and dynamic relationships between changing cultural preferences for family size and sex composition and the use of new reproductive technologies and abortion in realizing these preferences. It brings together both historical and contemporary forces that have shaped married couples preferences for family composition and have facilitated their access to and use of new reproductive technologies, especially ultrasonography. It shows that parents in Shahargaon—a rapidly urbanizing community near New Delhi—use ultrasonography to identify the sex of the fetus and practice female-selective abortion to avoid the birth of an unwanted daughter. Through personal stories and experiences of women and men in Shahargaon, the book shows that couples decisions to seek fetal knowledge and make decisions about female-selective abortion are informed by a host of interacting historical traditions, cultural practices, and emerging economic opportunities that have local, regional, and national underpinnings.

This book is unique in the sense that it is perhaps the first long-term ethnographic study on the use of ultrasonography for prenatal sex identification and the practice of female-selective abortion in India. Well-known slogans, such as "female feticide," "prenatal discrimination," "gendercide," and "missing women" have so far dominated the scholarly debate on the contentious issue of female-selective abortion. The slogans have played an important role in engaging researchers, activists, and policy makers in a constructive dialogue on the issue. I believe that, given the sensitivity and urgency of the topic, the debate has rapidly transformed into advocacy without the benefit of a well-researched, community-based understanding of why people choose to engage in such practices. I hope that my book fills this significant gap and constructively informs the ongoing debate on prenatal sex identification and female-selective abortion.

ACKNOWLEDGMENTS

Conducting ethnographic research on this issue has been one of the most challenging projects I have ever undertaken. One difficulty in carrying out community research has been the intimate, sensitive, and contentious nature of seeking information on fetal sex and abortion. Despite setbacks and frustrations throughout the fieldwork process, I remain convinced that a long-term systematic ethnographic approach is most suitable for studying a sensitive topic like this one. I accomplished the study with considerable help from my research assistants, women and men in Shahargaon, my family, and friends. I would like to extend my sincere gratitude to all of them.

My field trips to Shahargaon were funded by generous grants from the Wenner-Gren Foundation for Anthropological Research and the College of Liberal Arts, Oregon State University. Much of the archival research that contributed to the manuscript was funded by Library Research Travel Grants, Oregon State University.

Many people have contributed to the research and efforts for this book. I would like to thank all of them. I would especially like to thank John Young for encouraging me to undertake this writing project and for patiently making suggestions for improvements. Among my teachers at Syracuse University, Susan S. Wadley helped me develop a robust anthropological insight into studying my own society and introduced me to the rich ethnographic literature on India. She taught me how to think like an ethnographer. Several sections in the book are significantly revised and expanded versions of the articles previously published. I wish to gratefully acknowledge the publishers for allowing me to build upon my earlier work.

I dedicate this book to my parents, especially my mother, who taught me more lessons than I could remember, foremost among them being the importance of keeping an open mind and developing an informed outlook about the world.

Chapter 1

✳

Fieldwork on a Sensitive Issue

The idea for this book occurred to me in 1993, when I was conducting ethnographic research in Shahargaon—an urbanizing village located just south of New Delhi, India (Figure 1.1). Shahargaon (a pseudonym meaning "city-village") is a small village established by Haryana Jat migrants during the early eighteenth century. The name Shahargaon aptly describes a village community living at the fringes of a mega city amidst high-rise, residential, and commercial buildings. Just three decades ago, it was an isolated village having limited contact with the city. Today, the economy of Shahargaon has become integrated into that of the expanding metropolis of New Delhi. Shahargaon residents work in the surrounding urban market and are increasingly dependent on the city for everyday goods and services. For Shahargaon residents, the city provides economic opportunities and the village provides a sense of community and cultural continuity.

Shahargaon is numerically and politically dominated by the Jats—historically known as a dominant landowning subculture in north Indian society. Although a sizable body of anthropological literature has documented processes of cultural change in India, we know little about the positive and negative consequences of urbanization on Jat groups in north and northwestern India (Freed and Freed 1969, 1976, 1978, 1979; Lewis 1965).

In 1993, my ethnographic research project focused on son preference and daughter neglect in Shahargaon. For two months I had been collecting household census information and conducting in-depth interviews with key informants on why parents prefer sons over daughters. On one particularly hot and humid August day, I arrived at Dr. Mahavir Singh's clinic to conduct an interview. A Jat man in his mid-fifties, Dr. Singh practiced family medicine in the village. He met me at the front door and politely directed me to his office. It was a bright morning and, as we entered his office, it took a few moments for my eyes to adjust to the light. Gradually, I began to notice that Dr. Singh's office had a green curtain separating the patient waiting room from his messy desk, covered with medical texts and

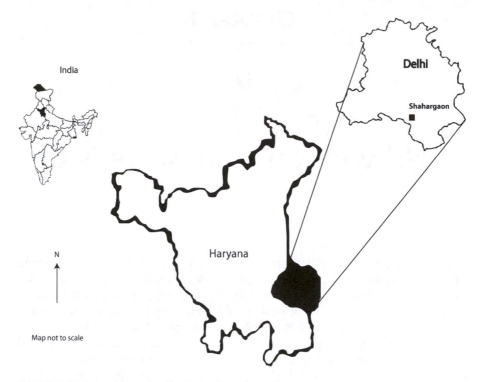

FIGURE 1.1   Map of India (© Sunil K. Khanna)

newspapers. A sphygmomanometer[1] and a stethoscope with worn-out tubing rested as decorative pieces on the left side of the table. The front end of the table top had a calendar acting as a marker separating the doctor's professional space on the table. A stool for patients stood at the right side of the table close to the doctor's chair. Dr. Singh's patients not only came from Shahargaon but also from neighboring villages and surrounding urban neighborhoods. He offered me a cup of hot Indian tea (*chai*). Just as we were about to begin our interview, a middle-aged gentleman lifted the green curtain and stuck in his head asking if it were possible to get an ultrasonography exam at Dr. Singh's clinic. Dr. Singh quickly offered him a chair and said, "Ultrasound [referring to an ultrasonography machine] is not available at this clinic, but I can refer you to a nearby specialty diagnostic clinic that has ultrasound. Tell me, when would you like your appointment?" "As soon as possible, the other doctor says it is already too late," the man nervously replied. Settling back in his chair Dr. Singh probed for further information: "Is it so? How late is it?" "It's my wife's fourth month," the man answered.

Seeming quite experienced in dealing with such situations, Dr. Singh responded in a reassuring manner: "Well, I do not think it is too late. I will speak with the doctor at the specialty clinic next door and arrange for everything you

---

1. A sphygmomanometer is an instrument commonly used by doctors to measure blood pressure. It consists of an inflatable cuff attached to a manometer to measure arterial pressure.

need. You can come tomorrow around 10:00 in the morning. I promise we will take care of your problem." "How much time will it take?" the man rapidly asked. "It only takes an hour for the procedure. She will be able to go home immediately after the procedure. I know she cannot be away from home for too long," Dr. Singh explained. The man paused to muster courage and inquired in a low voice: "And if we need to get an abortion (*bacha giravana*)?" Up to this point in the conversation, I pretended to be an uninterested observer who just happened to be present in the doctor's clinic. However, the last question made me uncomfortable. Perhaps, it was not the right time for me to be there because the doctor and patient needed to converse in privacy and with confidentiality. I could not shake off a nagging feeling that my presence was both unethical and unwarranted. However, neither the doctor nor the inquiring man seemed to mind. "Of course, even that can be arranged," Dr. Singh responded confidently. His tone indicated that the two procedures, ultrasound and abortion, were routine. "If we do need an abortion, how long will that take?" questioned the man. Dr. Singh responded:

> The abortion procedure will take just another hour and we deliver the best service in Delhi. We have qualified lady doctors. We are not like other clinics where untrained doctors, less qualified nurses, and local midwives (*dais*) perform these sensitive procedures. We are recognized in the area for providing top quality service and we are licensed by the government of India.

This explanation sounded more like a sales pitch, which not only resolved any apprehensions but also won over a new customer. Dr. Singh sympathetically inquired, "Tell me, how many daughters do you have?" "Two daughters," the man responded. In an agitated tone the man continued: "I think if this time it is a girl we should go for an abortion and then try again. Hopefully, next time it will be boy." After the customary haggling over price, the two parties settled for a "reasonable" cost of 1500 rupees (approximately $36) for the ultrasound and 1000 rupees (approximately $24) for the abortion. The man left the clinic promising to return the next day.

RESEARCH VERSUS ADVOCACY

The above narrative frames the purpose of this book—to understand why some parents in India use ultrasonography to identify the sex of the fetus and seek sexselective abortion of female fetuses. Previous to the above encounter, I had read journal articles and newspapers reporting on the use and "misuse" of new reproductive technologies (NRTs), primarily ultrasonography and amniocentesis. This was the first time I had witnessed negotiations between a client and a doctor to arrange for diagnosis of fetal sex and abortion services. The accounts I had read almost all agree that preference for sons is the key to explaining why married couples selectively abort female fetuses (Croll 2000; Ghosh 2005; Sharma 2006). They describe son preference as a historically intrinsic characteristic of Indian society. These accounts raise awareness about an important issue, but they also err in giving the impression that preference for sons is an ancient cultural characteristic "unchanged" or "frozen in time." The key question, addressed by only a few researchers, is why son preference continues to exist and what contemporary forces contribute to parents' decisions to use new reproductive technologies (Jeffery et al. 1984; Khanna 1997; Unisa et al. 2003).

Recently, several scholars and policy makers have suggested that urbanization may lead to a decline in son preference (Chung and Das Gupta 2007). Although important because of its policy implications, researchers have not tested this assertion in the Indian context. One reason for the limited attention to this question is that the debate on ultrasonography and female-selective abortion rapidly turned into advocacy without the benefit of a well-researched, community-based understanding of why people choose to engage in such practices. Activists and intellectuals both in India and abroad were too quick to express their condemnation on moral and ethical grounds.

One difficulty in carrying out research on son preference and sex-selective abortion is the intimate and sensitive nature of the topic. Spending time and building trust is the only way to develop a nuanced understanding of long established cultural traditions and to become familiar with the local realities that people face in their everyday lives. This kind of research requires being sensitive not only to individual concerns about privacy and confidentiality, but also to the rights of the larger community.

An ethnographic approach is suitable for studying sensitive topics because it primarily relies on qualitative methods—participant observation and open-ended interviews. In my research in Shahargaon I combined participant observation and open-ended interviews with other methods, including household surveys, family genealogies, structured interviews, and focus group interviews.

FIELDWORK EXPERIENCE

Shahargaon is a typical north Indian village experiencing rapid urbanization. Since 1993, I have completed six fieldwork-based studies broadly on the topic of son preference and daughter neglect among married couples in Shahargaon. My relationship with the Shahargaon community is ongoing and I continue to return there. My first project examined son preference and daughter neglect focusing on the impact of selective discrimination against girls on their growth and overall health status. On this trip I conducted a household census collecting demographic data and family genealogies. In 1996, I completed an ethnographic study on opinions regarding the ideal family size and sex composition among married Jat couples in Shahargaon. The study focused on the awareness, availability, and use of ultrasonography for prenatal sex identification and the practice of female-selective abortion. During 1999–2001, I returned to Shahargaon twice to conduct

TABLE 1.1 **Shahargaon's Population according to Caste Affiliation**
(2003 Census; Native Shahargaon residents only)

Social Groups	Households	Population
Brahman (Priest)	5	27
Jat (Agriculturalist)	179	938
Kumhar (Potter)	5	28
Nai (Barber)	15	92
Chamar (Leatherworker)	13	91
Harijan (Sweeper)	28	160
Total	245	1336

an in-depth study on family-building strategies. In 1999, I conducted another household census survey. Then I made two short field trips in 2003 and 2005. In 2003, I conducted the most recent village household census and also collected information on household economic status. Relative to the population of other villages in the region, Shahargaon is small. According to my 2003 household census, Shahargaon's population of native residents (not including renters) is 1336 (245 households), including 938 Jats (179 households). Thus, the Jats constitute a numerical and political majority in the village. The remaining 66 families belong to non-Jat groups (Table 1.1). In Table 1.1, I have arranged social groups according to the villagers' perception of social hierarchy.

I took every opportunity to talk with people casually while they were working in their homes or shops, while they were relaxing and enjoying a mid-day break with friends and neighbors. The best places to meet people were the village markets, where they went to buy, sell, or simply "hang out." Another common meeting place was the village council office, where men gathered to discuss local politics or to play cards and chess. My everyday interaction with villagers afforded me an opportunity to observe behavior in its natural context, and listen to candid opinions on various topics of local importance. I conducted numerous in-depth interviews with married women and men, community leaders, local doctors, and activists who opposed prenatal sex identification (Figure 1.2). I kept detailed notes on the background of the individuals I was observing and interviewing.

NATIVE ANTHROPOLOGIST

Being a "native anthropologist" born in India and trained in the United States, I had the advantage of the ability to speak several local languages and to possess familiarity with mannerisms and customs commonly associated with north Indian communities. However, my status as a "native" posed challenges, especially in establishing relationships and conducting interviews. Often informants skipped over details expecting me to fill in the gaps on my own. My questions often generated varying expressions of irritation, disbelief, and amazement. When I asked for missing details, they would scoff at me, "Of course, you should know the answer yourself." The village midwife once scolded me for asking questions

FIGURE 1.2   Sunil Khanna with Dalbir, a Jat man in his mid-forties (© Sunil K. Khanna)

which even "a child would not ask." Some identified me as a "city boy" (*shahri babu*), a foreigner (*firangi*), a foreigner-Indian (*desi-firangi*), or even a city-Indian-foreigner (*firangi-desi*). My identity in the field was neither fixed nor under my control. I did not carry the well-defined and bounded label of an anthropologist in the field. For some Shahargaon residents, I was a student learning about health issues. For others, I was an Indian who was visiting Shahargaon to conduct a village census (*jān ganana*). Often my research assistants introduced me as an "America–returned–scientist" (*vaigyanic jo amreka ghum kar aye hain*). They regarded my experience abroad as symbolic of wisdom, maturity, and success, although I still carried the stigma of an ignorant "urbanite" (*shahri*). I was an expert from abroad whose interests and manners were slightly different but interesting.

The truth is that I did not already know the answers to my questions. Although I grew up nearby in New Delhi, this was my first extended experience with everyday village life in India. While growing up in an urban environment, my interaction was mostly limited to my immediate neighborhood. I rarely ventured out to sample village life, since I had no inclination to do so until I became an anthropologist and began to understand the importance of ethnography in addressing social issues.

Fieldwork in Shahargaon forced me to reflect upon my own ambiguous position—was I a native anthropologist studying my own society, or was I an urban outsider studying an unfamiliar rural culture? I experienced a heightened awareness of my own feelings, biases, and limitations. My field notes were often burdened with reflexive passages of how I felt while interviewing my fellow

Indians. At times, I felt a sense of confusion or lack of understanding about what was going on around me. On other occasions, I felt frustrated with my inability to correctly answer the questions posed to me by my research participants. According to them, I should have known the answers to their questions. In several instances I doubted my purpose of being in Shahargaon collecting information and data on the personal lives of my fellow Indians.

Being a native of India, I also felt an enhanced sense of responsibility toward my informants. Conducting fieldwork became an exercise in how to balance my need for collection information with the individual need for privacy and sensitivity in discussing their family situations. As I started writing about my experiences in Shahargaon, presenting information in a manner that is most respectful of the privacy of my informants became a challenge about what to present and what to keep confidential. National or cultural identity evoking either pride or disaffection, or both, also enters into such decisions. I had to keep in mind that in an increasingly interconnected world, considerations of class, ethnicity, and gender extend across national boundaries. Instead of the simple dichotomy of native versus outsider, these characteristics and shared experiences play an important role in defining sameness and difference.

ENTERING SHAHARGAON

During my first visit to Shahargaon in 1993, Sohan Lal, the village council chief, carefully scrutinized my intentions in selecting his village for study. I wanted to impress him favorably because he was a respected elder in the village and people listened to him. Typically, a village or group of villages elects a local governing political council of five members (*Panchayat*) for a minimum period of three years. The council members elect a council chief and take a leadership role in becoming a political voice for the village community, engaging in community welfare programs and activities, managing infrastructure, resolving minor intra-village disputes, and serving as role models for others in the village. A village council is expected to cover 10,000 people and may extend its jurisdiction to neighboring villages. Shahargaon's village council is responsible for four additional villages in the vicinity. In 1993, the Shahargaon community had elected five Jat men to the village council. Women rarely participated in the activities of the village council. Jat men controlled much of the political and social welfare activities in the village. Strong cultural barriers, including gender bias, restrictions on women's mobility, and women's household responsibilities, severely limited their participation in political and public activities in the village.

Our first meeting was in the village council office. I showed him a letter I had received from the Block Development Office (BDO) in New Delhi requesting that the village council allow me to conduct research in Shahargaon (Figure 1.3). He carefully read the letter and in a stern voice asked me, "Why do you want to conduct your research in our village?" I replied, "My research can be best accomplished in a small village experiencing urbanization. I feel that Shahargaon best fits that criterion." He then proceeded to ask me a series of questions about

FIGURE 1.3   Village Council Meeting in Progress (© Sunil K. Khanna)

the people I would be interested in interviewing. I answered that I was interested in learning about how Shahargaon's culture is changing as a result of its contact with urban New Delhi. He followed with another question, "What do you plan to do with this information?" I told him that I would write an account of village life and, perhaps someday, even publish a book. Sohan Lal appeared visibly impressed, and proceeded to tell me that life in Shahargaon was changing quite rapidly:

> I am afraid that we will forget our ways, especially our children and grandchildren. I very much appreciate your work here and hope that it can be of some use to us in teaching our children about the village. Our children are so impressed with New Delhi (*Nai Dilli*). They forget that before all this happened Shahargaon was here and that when all this is over Shahargaon will be here. It is their village.

I must admit, I was surprised by Sohan Lal's comments (Figure 1.4). In spite of his abrupt questioning and domineering demeanor towards me, he understood the purpose of my research much better than I was able to articulate in the midst of my anxiety to gain his support.

After my interview with Sohan Lal, I waited outside the village council room while the council members debated the reason for my presence and whether or

F I G U R E 1.4   Sohan Lal, Chief of the Village Council (© Sunil K. Khanna)

not they would give me to permission to conduct research in their village. The meeting lasted for about two rounds of tea (*chai*), after which Sohan Lal emerged to inform me that the council had granted permission for my study on the condition that I follow the council's orders about my living situation. I had no choice about choosing a place to live. The council arranged for me to live with Raghvir's family because they deemed his place as suitable for an "urban resident" (*shahri*) who had to do a lot of reading and writing (Figure 1.5). They settled on the amount of monthly rent and payments for food and other services without even asking for my opinion. I had to pay a certain amount and that was it. Raghvir's family, including his elderly parents, wife, two sons and a daughter, lived in a two-story house considered big by Shahargaon standards.

It had well maintained concrete floors and a painted cement exterior. On my first visit to the house, his wife Bala showed me the room that she had set aside for me on the main floor. She proudly pointed to the electric outlets for my tape recorder, laptop, and battery chargers.

Before long I encountered family level politics, discovering that my assigned residence meant that I could not visit certain houses or talk with or behave in a friendly manner toward some members in the community. I also had to avoid asking certain types of questions that made people uncomfortable. My initial confusion about these restrictions confirmed I was the "ignorant" urbanite (*shahri*) who did not understand the "rural world" (*dehat*). However, I soon found that the

FIGURE 1.5   Raghvir (© Sunil K. Khanna)

restrictions were helpful during the initial phase of my fieldwork. Establishing rapport in the field is a delicate and risky process. I realized that given the intense politics in the village, I had plenty of opportunities to make serious mistakes and only a few moments to get things right. Until I figured out appropriate ways of behaving, the restrictions helped me in avoiding mistakes and in presenting myself in an acceptable manner.

My camera was particularly helpful making friends and getting to know families. My enthusiasm for photography facilitated my initial breakthrough in establishing rapport, as villagers invited me to numerous family events and celebrations to take pictures and later share them with family members. By so doing I earned the respected title of "village photographer."

LONG-TERM FIELDWORK

My work in Shahargaon has now spanned more than a decade. During this time, I have become close to some village men and women who assigned me different kinship statuses in their families. I am an uncle (*chacha*) to the married and unmarried children of my host family, a brother (*bhai*) to young women, and a son (*beta*) to a domineering, elderly woman named Jati who enjoys watching me eat spicy food. Hetram, the ever-silent patriarch of a powerful Jat family, at first avoided me, but after several years he began to regard me as a son and told me great stories about Shahargaon's history and his life as a peasant agriculturalist during his youth. "You keep coming back to this village; you are either very serious about your work or you do not have anything better to do," he jokingly remarked during an interview in 2003.

Anthropologists conducting long-term fieldwork in a village community experience changes over time in the way their research participants perceive them (Srinivas 1976; Wadley 1994). Community members construct multiple identities of the ethnographer based on their experience and understanding of ethnographic encounters. These identities continuously change as more interaction occurs. Meanwhile anthropologists learn and adapt to the complexities of local politics and power differences. As I became accustomed to the nuances of inter-household and village politics in Shahargaon, I was better able to manage my behavior and interaction with informants. Perhaps as a result, many of them relaxed the restrictions they had imposed on me during my first extended stay in the village. For example, early in my fieldwork, villagers asked me to wait outside the house while my research assistants conducted interviews with Jat women. Later, women participants insisted that I enter their homes and conduct the interviews myself. They wanted me to hear their stories firsthand. Sometimes they even reminded me to check if the tape recorder was working and asked me to replay parts of the recorded conversation to make sure that their views were properly recorded.

On later visits to the village I also found that both men and women began to respond positively to my questions on sensitive topics, especially those related to household income, conception, contraception, pregnancy, childbirth, abortion, and decision-making processes about family-building strategies in their households. They also wanted to know about my family background, occupation, and life in the United States. My interviews thus evolved into much longer two-way exchanges of information in a more comfortable kind of interaction. For example, in group interviews informants often turned the same questions back to me, asking if I had children and if my sisters or other family members had experienced miscarriages or abortions. My experience is typical of what happens in long-term fieldwork—the anthropologist finds that "short and sketchy" interviews over time become "long and interactive," as the anthropologist and the informant learn about each other.

In the later stages of my fieldwork, interviews typically began with amusing talk before they turned serious. Group interviews contained giggles, jokes, and small talk throughout the session, and afforded an opportunity for the women to catch up in discussing family matters and village politics. My interest in conception, pregnancy, and childbirth led to several embarrassing situations. On more than one occasion I became a source of amusement for Jat women. For example, one day I visited an informant who had recently given birth to a son. Her excited mother-in-law offered me what looked like a pastry (*gond* or *ladoo*). She explained that if I wanted to learn about pregnancy and childbirth I must eat it. Reluctantly and sensing that she was making a joke at my expense, I ate the gummy confection, which had a strong sweet taste and was so sticky that I found it hard to chew and swallow. I felt choked, and at that moment the expression of panic and fear along with embarrassment on my face became a source of laughter for everyone present in the room. The special food item (*gond* or *ladoo*), I learned later, is a common prescription for a woman who has just delivered a baby. It includes cumin, edible plant latex and gum, almonds, raisins, fennel, cardamom, brown sugar, wheat flour, and purified butter. The Jats believe that it increases breast milk production, restores bodily energy, and helps repair internal tissue damage due to childbirth. Because I am a man, the women found my interviewing to be a source of amusement. Not accustomed to men showing interest in women's re- productive issues, they regarded the experience of answering my questions to be out of the ordinary and delighted in making jokes about it.

A CHANGING COMMUNITY

The agrarian cultural characteristics associated with Shahargaon's past greatly in- fluence the village community's relationship with the present. For more than two centuries after establishing the village, Jat families have practiced and preserved their traditional rural way of life. Before the early 1970s, Shahargaon remained an isolated village having little or no contact either with New Delhi or other com- munities outside of their historical network of kinsmen. Shahargaon Jats only infrequently ventured out to trade their agricultural produce in the wholesale market town of Mandi, just a few miles to the southeast. Now, almost 35 years after urban expansion into Shahargaon, agricultural work has all but died, yet the peasant tradition continues to define and shape the community and its environs. I chose this community for study because it exemplifies a typical agrarian settle- ment experiencing urban assimilation. It is no longer an insular place, as it is intricately linked to urban networks of commerce and government, and also to other communities in the larger region.

   Using Shahargaon as an illustrative case, this book examines how urbanization affects a peasant community's social and cultural characteristics, especially those associated with marriage, conception, and family building. Communities in north India, such as the Jats, historically have exhibited strong preference for sons over daughters, which many observers believe is the root cause of female feticide in north India. However, the Shahargaon case is one of continuing change requiring new or modified explanations grounded in and relevant to the everyday circum- stances and experiences of people living in that community. Culture is dynamic and changes over time as communities adapt to and reshape both external and internal forces.

APPLIED ANTHROPOLOGY IN A CHANGING WORLD

I have written this book at a time when anthropology, having emerged stronger from the challenges it faced in the last three decades, is becoming a significant voice in the policy debate surrounding issues such as abortion, population control, new reproductive technologies, illegal trafficking of human organs, environmental degradation, indigenous knowledge, migration, ethnic conflict, globalization, health, and many more policy-related issues. This trend in anthropological research requires inclusive, interdisciplinary, and application-oriented approaches. Anthropologists today are interested not only in critiquing existing canons of knowledge, but also in seeking creative means to contribute toward programs and policies related to improving the human condition. At this crucial point in the development of our discipline, the state of anthropology is optimistically oriented toward the application of anthropological knowledge to human affairs. This prospective and important sentiment is most clearly spelled out in the 2000 American Anthropological Association's (AAA) annual meeting theme in which President Louise Lamphere aptly remarks that the very first AAA meeting in the new millennium will explore:

> the many ways in which anthropological knowledge can be directed toward educating both public and private sectors and in disseminating critical information to policy makers, decision makers, and opinion makers on a variety of issues (*Lamphere 2000:48*).

The above theme statement reflects more than just the agenda. It firmly proposes a direction for research, teaching, and training in anthropology. Intriguingly, this proposal for anthropology's future recognizes the leading role of applied anthropology (and practicing anthropology in non-academic settings), and strongly advocates a commitment toward the application of anthropological knowledge. While we may disagree on anthropology's ethical obligations and moral responsibilities, it is imperative for us to understand recognize that our on-the-ground research and access to unique information can inform us about others and help facilitate culturally sensitive social change (Comaroff 2006). The insider (emic) perspective is missing from the policy context and ethnographic investigation can supply it.

The debate on the use of ultrasonography for prenatal sex identification and female feticide in India demands a similar commitment from anthropologists. In dealing with an issue so sensitive and contentious, I have benefited much from insights gained from the tools and perspectives developed by applied anthropologists. Here I describe people's everyday experiences, their stories, dreams, frustrations, confusions, and deliberations about important issues in their lives, and I show how decision-making in their households is linked to the interconnected arenas of socio-economic change, government regulations, and increasing demands of a rapidly globalizing world.

I have resisted labeling the practice of female feticide as "gendercide" or "genocide of women," not because I disagree with the sentiments expressed by these slogans, but because I believe such slogans invoke a strong emotional response and focus attention on a trend toward alarmism in Indian society. Such slogans often create arbitrary dichotomies—men versus women, tradition versus modernization, and patriarchy versus women's rights, which often obfuscate the real considerations involved in decision-making processes at the village level. In order to understand the use and "misuse" of ultrasonography, we must develop a clear understanding of people's values, opinions, and experiences. Whether or not "misuse" is a proper term depends on the views of the people studied, not on the judgment of society. This ethnographic account describes the everyday circumstances in which married couples make decisions related to their family size and sex composition in a community historically known for a strong preference for sons. They do not make these decisions in a historical vacuum, but neither are they divorced from the everyday realities of rapid urbanization experienced by their community. Specifically in this case study, I focus on the following questions about India in general and the Shahargaon Jat community in particular:

1. Why does son preference still persist?
2. What is the desired family size and sex composition?
3. Why are new reproductive technologies popular?
4. Has government regulation of the availability and use of new reproductive technologies been effective in preventing prenatal sex selection?
5. What strategies can be effective in curbing the "misuse" of ultrasonography and preventing female-selective abortion?

I hope that addressing the above questions will help shape the ongoing debate among scholars, activists, and policy makers about cultural mediation in the definition and use of reproductive technologies, the regulation of these technologies, the traditions and practices associated with reproduction in urbanizing communities, the global forces bringing about change, and how national population control and other policies impact the use of new reproductive technologies.

Chapter 2

✴

Shahargaon: "The Village of My Ancestors"

Doing ethnographic research demands patience and consistency. It is a slow and gradual process. My ethnographic research was slow, perhaps frustratingly slower than I had anticipated before arriving in Shahargaon. I had been in the village for almost three months and I was still playing the role of the village photographer. The only progress I had made was to have initiated a household census in the village. I was beginning to question my method of gaining entry into the village. Did I make a mistake by breaking a cardinal rule of village life? Why were not many people interested in talking to me? What was I doing in this village anyway? Is it ethical of me to expect that people will take the time to talk to me and answer my mundane, and perhaps silly, questions? Why should they talk to me? I am here because I want to begin a career as an anthropologist. But what are they getting for talking to me? Am I being a selfish researcher? A sense of panic was beginning to set in, making me feel that my research was going nowhere. The slow progress of my fieldwork was making me question my training and ability as an ethnographer. Perhaps, I was not cut out be an anthropologist. Perhaps, it was time for me to look for another profession.

The best decision I made in the field was at this critical juncture; I chose to stick to my routine. Notwithstanding a growing sense of urgency, I tried as much as possible to keep a smiling face and hide the combined feelings of panic, insecurity, and frustration. During early months, my two research assistants were my only two sources of information about the village. They not only served as key informants, but also helped me in collecting genealogies and household census information. Gradually, people became used to my presence and allowed me to enter their homes to collect household information. Every morning I would meet with my research assistants at the local tea stall (*dhaba*) to count the number of completed genealogies and household census forms, check for errors, and cross-check census information. At the end of our meeting, we would plan our day and visit people in their homes. Often we had to visit the same home numerous times to complete the household survey forms. Although villagers treated me with respect, they considered me to be an outsider, and much of the information they provided was perfunctory and superficial. It was hard for me to engage with someone in a deeper discussion regarding son preference and daughter neglect. Reluctantly, I accepted the limitations placed on me and continued my work believing that eventually a good ethnographer will be able to piece together disparate strands of information in a coherent narrative. I knew that I could succeed by maintaining cultural relativism—examining cultures in their own contexts—and avoiding ethnocentrism—using one's own preconceived cultural values to judge other cultures (Fadorak 2007).

Members of the Shahargaon community gradually accepted me into the community. As weeks turned into months, individuals started inviting me into their homes for tea or lunch. They would often stop me in the alleyways to talk to me. The casual conversations invariably turned into discussions and then into formal structured interviews. My numerous discussions with Jat women helped me formulate an understanding about the relationship between women and men in the village, son preference and daughter neglect, marriage preferences, and the role of women during the agricultural days in Shahargaon. I also collected detailed reproductive histories of Jat women, including information on number of conceptions, failed pregnancies, and births. This historical information later proved helpful in understanding the reproductive choices made by Shahargaon Jat parents in the present.

In addition to using participant observation and unstructured interviews in ethnographic research, anthropologists have long relied on retrospective research methods to collect information about the past, especially about individual experiences and important events in their lives. These methods have received much attention in feminist anthropology, especially in a patriarchal context where women's words and stories have been traditionally muted (Gluck and Patai 1991). I have used these methods in collecting information about women's experiences in Shahargaon, with the goal of allowing their words and understandings to predominate and correct any male bias in my research. As a male researcher I found that collecting Jat women's reproductive histories was not an easy task. Although this information was vital to my work, I waited patiently for long periods of time until people felt comfortable talking with me. Raghvir and Bala, my host family in the village, suggested that I hire Jat women as my research assistants to collect reproductive histories. Given the sensitive and private nature of the information, I decided to follow this advice. Although marred by slow progress, my approach approved to be effective in the long run. Jat women openly shared their experiences with my research assistants and gradually became accustomed to my presence in the group. Our interview sessions with women often turned into group interviews as other women from the same extended family or neighborhood came and joined the conversation (Figure 2.1).

During these sessions, women repeatedly corrected each other to achieve accuracy in reporting numbers, timing, and the outcome of individual pregnancies. They recalled individual reproductive histories, narrated one or two specific stories associated with pregnancy and childbirth, and questioned and corrected

F I G U R E 2.1   Jat women participating in a group interview session (© Sunil K. Khanna)

each other according to their individual interpretations of the events. Some researchers believe that collecting retrospective reproductive histories is fraught with inaccuracies due to faulty memory or bias. In my experience, Shahargaon Jat women vividly remembered not only their own reproductive histories but also those of other women in the village. The exercise of gathering retrospective data based on collective memories proved to be an effective mechanism to correct for the shortcomings of individual retrospection.

JAT CHARACTERISTICS

I learned different meanings of the word "Jat" during several discussions with Mohinder Singh, a 65-year-old village man, who observed that Jats felt a sense of pride about themselves—a sense that echoed their hardworking peasant life and an indomitable spirit. "We are Jat, which means we stand for justice, we are full of aggression, and we believe in telling the truth," he explained. Then he continued with more details:

> My people have fought great battles against the Muslim rulers and the British. Although they ruled India, they were unable to rule the Jats. Our conversation style and mannerism can be crass and insulting to non-Jat people and that is why they call us the just-avoid-them-people.

Historians have expressed multiple views on the meaning of the word "Jat" and the origins of the Jats as an important agricultural community. According to Westphal-Hellbusche and Westphal (1964), the Arabic equivalent of Jat is *Zutt*, a generic term used for "men from India." The word also means "bunch of hair," and the Jats themselves claim that they have descended from the hair of Shiva,[1] one of the three key Hindu deities. According to Ibbetson (1916), Jats are of Indo-Aryan (or Indo-Scythian) descent. Bowles (1977) suggests that the word Jat in the Punjabi language means a "grazer" or "herdsman," but notes Ibbetson's (1916) observation that a shift from the Punjabi soft "t" to a hard "t" in some Muslim communities changes the meaning to "Jat agriculturalist." The writings of British officers and missionaries describe the Jats as revenue-payers par excellence who are also sturdy and independent. These accounts reported that the Jats constituted a "bold peasantry with pride accustomed to guide the plough and wield the sword with equal readiness and success—second to no other Indian race in hard work or courage" (Qanungo 1925:1).

Geographic Distribution, Caste Ranking, and Religion

According to recent population estimates, the total population of Jats in South Asia is roughly 30 million. This population projection is based on information collected during the 1931 Census, which was the last to report caste affiliation. At that time an estimated 8 million Jats lived mostly in India and Pakistan.

The current estimates are proportional projections based on the region's total population growth. The Jats are distributed over a wide and diverse geographic area—from the hot and humid regions in northwestern India to the hills and plains in southern Pakistan—and exhibit extensive cultural, linguistic, and religious diversity (Figure 2.2).[2] Jats constitute one of the largest and most diverse communities living in northwestern India and Pakistan. Different Jat groups living in this vast region speak different dialects of Hindi, Urdu, Sindhi, and Punjabi. Despite this variation, Datta (2000) observes that the present-day Jat agriculturalists and pastoralists in North India share distinct socio-cultural and religious practices.

Assigning a social ranking to the Hindu Jats has been a contentious issue as scholars have disagreed on the historical position of the community. Traditionally, Hindu society is organized into four hierarchical groups called the *varnas*. The four *varnas* are listed here in order of social rank from the highest to the lowest—Priests (*Brahmans*), Warriors (*Kshatriyas*), Traders or Producers (*Vaishyas*), and Menial Workers (*Shudras*). This ranking constituted the core principle of Hindu social organization. Each caste or occupational group is affiliated with one of the four *varna* categories which defines their status. Scholars have pointed out that the *varna* categories constitute a normative or prescriptive view of social hierarchy and that local communities may not strictly adhere to this view of social life (Singer 1972).

---

1. In Hinduism, Shiva is also known as "the lord of the animals" (*Pashupati*) or the Lord of the Cosmic Dance (*Natraj*). Hindus believe that Shiva holds the divine power of the natural world, including that of rivers and animals. Shiva is also called a "destroyer."

2. Outlying Jat groups also inhabit distant regions as the Maldives, Russia, and Ukraine.

Distribution of Jats in South Asia

FIGURE 2.2 Map showing distribution of Jats in South Asia (© Sunil K. Khanna)

Throughout the 1900s, Jat leaders and academic scholars have associated the Jats with different *varna* categories. Some have identified the Jats as belonging to the warrior group, whereas others have argued that they belonged to the "menial worker group" (Bowles 1977; Datta 2000; Qanungo 1925). Freed and Freed (1993) point out that well into the 1970s the Jats constitute a major landowning community in northwestern India. The Jats have often used their dominant economic and political status to define themselves as belonging to a high *varna* ranking. However, over the years several Jat communities have abandoned agriculture and chosen to support themselves by taking urban jobs. These recent economic changes have once again challenged the much contested *varna* status of the Jat community. According to a report published in *The Hindustan Times* (October 18th, 1999), the Delhi Commission for Other Backward Classes (OBC) recommended that the Jats living in New Delhi be included in the OBC list as they constituted an economically backward caste. This recommendation was based on the results of a survey showing that Jats living in New Delhi existed at a low level of social, economic, and educational development.

The Jats in India primarily practice Hindu religion. Hindu Jat communities follow *Arya Samaj*—a reform sect founded by Swami Dayanand Saraswati in the mid-1800s. By affiliating with this reform sect, the Jat community acquired "…textual sophistication, uniformity, and internal mechanisms for marshalling intellectual resources" (Datta 2000:48). In western Punjab, which is now part of

Pakistan, the Jat community adopted Islam between 8th and 10th centuries. Some Jat communities in Punjab and other north Indian states, including Haryana and Uttar Pradesh, follow Sikh religion. One of the five major religious traditions in India, the Sikh religion emerged as a major spiritual force in the 15th century. Its founder, Guru Nanak, preached the idea of universal love and advocated equality for all regardless of caste, class, color, or gender. During the 17th century, influenced by the message of social equality and by political and economic needs of the period, a number of Jat communities embraced Sikh religion. These groups are called "Jat Sikhs."

THE STORY OF SHAHARGAON

I collected different pieces of the historical information presented in this chapter from several field visits to Shahargaon. Among the Shahargaon Jats, there are considerable differences of opinions regarding the history of the village. Therefore, developing a coherent history of Shahargaon proved to be a formidable task akin to solving a complex jigsaw puzzle. Shahargaon's history spanning almost 250 years is not available in any written publication and only exists primarily through memory and oral transmission. I interviewed several villagers—women and men, young and old—asking for their recollections of Shahargaon's beginnings, past, and present transition as an urbanizing community. I recorded and analyzed the stories they recounted and their memories of events either as directly experienced or as passed down to them by their parents and grandparents. Each villager narrated a slightly different version of village history. Sometimes these versions were influenced by external events or secondary sources of information. Their recollections also proved to be quite different from a widely shared "popular" version of Shahargaon's history. From these subjective accounts, I tried to piece together a collective history of the village. I quickly realized that the different versions were irreconcilable. Nevertheless, the process of collecting historical data proved to be a useful means of learning about how people in the village defined themselves and interpreted their past, especially as they embraced the idea that they no longer lived in an insular village. An added benefit of this exercise was that people became interested in talking to me.

Purgaon to Shahargaon

My quest for an authoritative source on Shahargaon's history finally ended when Sohan Lal told me that I should speak with Om Prakash (Figure 2.3), a Jat man in his sixties who is also the head of one of the most affluent families in the village. I met Om Prakash on my third visit to his house.

He was busy running a construction materials shop. "I must not fail this time and make sure that I interview him," I mumbled to myself as I knocked on his door. Om Prakash opened the door and asked me to follow him to the back of his house. He led me into a small, stuffy room dimly lit by a ceiling lamp. I could see

FIGURE 2.3   Om Prakash (© Sunil K. Khanna)

that he had already been sifting through folders with irregularly stapled sets of pages, some of which were curling at the margins. He pointed toward the folders and said, "This is the history of Shahargaon, the village of my ancestors."

He conveyed a sense of pride in his voice called himself a proud member of the Shahargaon Jat community. I explained to him that I was interested learning about changes over time with regard to village lifestyle, subsistence patterns, son preference, and family characteristics. The interview quickly turned into a long monologue by Om Prakash, interrupted only briefly by a few of my leading questions. According to Om Prakash, Shahargaon has two major historical periods. The first (pre-1970s) agricultural period came before the Delhi Development Authority (DDA) confiscated village agricultural land as part of its urban expansion project. The second (post-1970s) urbanization period originated from increased urban contact and resulted in a shift away from an agricultural way of life. Approximately 250 years ago four Jat brothers founded Shahargaon. They came from Purgaon, a village in Haryana located approximately 75 miles to the west.

The four brothers had less farm land than other families in Purgaon. Occasionally they traveled long distances to sell surplus crops in the urban markets of New Delhi. Shahargaon was located along their trade route, a journey two days from their home village. When a wealthy Muslim landlord offered to sell the Shahargaon area, the Jat brothers saw an opportunity to obtain larger landholdings and improve their economic status. They hoped to maintain their agricultural way of life while taking advantage of the better trading opportunities made possible by the strategic location of their new village. Eventually, they brought their families and attached service caste families from Haryana to settle in Shahargaon.[3]

Since Om Prakash's narrative was concise and clear, I did not get the impression that he was trying to hide any unpleasant facts about Shahargaon's history. However, a competing version of Shahargaon's beginnings claims that the four original Jat brothers attacked and occupied an already established village settlement, and then struck a deal with the Muslim landlord, who reluctantly agreed to sell the village land at an affordable price. Elder members of the village, including Om Prakash, reject this version of the story, strongly asserting that their ancestors were not violent and that their village was not founded by means of treachery, deceit, or violence.

THE PRE-1970S PERIOD

The region of New Delhi, which includes the neighboring states of Haryana, Punjab, and Uttar Pradesh, constitutes the main territory of the Jats. Numerous Jat village settlements line the west and south-west borders of New Delhi. The Jats are known locally as chiefs (*chowdharies*)—a title that symbolizes leadership derived from their ancestral control over land and socioeconomic dominance (Pradhan 1966).

A typical Jat village consists of one or two compact housing settlements surrounded by agricultural land and pasture for livestock (Figure 2.4). Compared to other Jat villages on the borders of New Delhi, Shahargaon is the smallest and the most recently established. Regional folklore and proverbs emphasize the community's agricultural and pastoral past and its ancestral attachment to land. Shahargaon Jats farmed staple cereal crops such as wheat, maize, and millet, and cash crops such as sugarcane, fruits, and vegetables. The numerical majority of Jats over members of service caste families in the village facilitated their continuing dominance of the economic and sociopolitical aspects of village life.

The preference for sons over daughters in Indian society is stronger in the north than in the south. Differences in cultural traditions and practices associated with the ownership and inheritance of property, decision-making power both within and outside the household, marriage patterns, participation in rituals, and

---

3. In a traditional north Indian village, several lower caste families perform daily services associated with cleaning, hair cutting, washing clothes, and farming for upper caste or landowning families. Service caste families performed essential functions to the survival of a traditional village community.

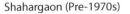

Shahargaon (Pre-1970s)

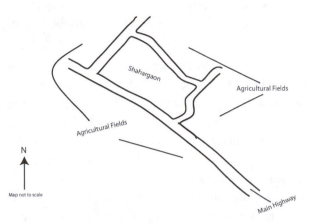

FIGURE 2.4   Shahargaon area before the 1970s (© Sunil K. Khanna)

old-age security are central to explaining this phenomenon (Agarwal 1994; Croll 2000; Mines and Lamb 2002). Peasant communities in the north need sons as laborers for farming the land and as a security force for defending against encroachment over local land boundaries. They practice village exogamy, marrying outside one's birth village, and patrilocal residence, where a daughter leaves her parents' home after marriage to live with her husband's family in another village. At the time of her marriage, the daughter's parents must give money and gifts as dowry to the groom's family. After her marriage she does not contribute economically to her parents' family. For this reason parents often perceive daughters as an economic liability or a drain on family resources. In contrast, the marriage of a son means that his parents receive gifts and money from the bride's family. The son will continue to live with his parents, carry on the family name, and inherit the family property. Since he provides economic security and support, his parents consider him to be a valuable asset in enhancing the family's well-being, security, prestige, and political influence.

Consistent with the North Indian cultural pattern of male dominance, Jat households (*ghar*) trace their descent to a common male ancestor or lineage (*kunba*). In anthropological terms, they represent a patrilineal society in which family name and inheritance of property pass through the male line. The Jat community in Shahargaon traces its descent from a single clan, namely the Malik clan (*gotra*). In local parlance, Shahargaon is a common clan village (*sagota gaon*) or a "village of Maliks" (*Malikon ka gaon*). The Malik Jat community in Haryana traditionally occupied a higher economic, ritual, and numerical status than other clans in the region (Mann 1988). However, as new immigrants, the Shahargaon Jats faced considerable hardship during the early settlement period and suffered a loss of social status with respect to neighboring Jat villages. According to Om Prakash, the first few Jat generations in Shahargaon were in a struggle for survival. Although they had migrated seeking prosperity, their hopes for a better life were not immediately realized. The rocky terrain and high elevation of the village land made water a scarce resource. In the early settlement period, agriculture in Shahargaon was labor intensive and irrigation water was scarce. A good harvest was a rare event. Families suffered from constant food shortages and barely met their subsistence needs. According to Om Prakash:

> Farming in Shahargaon was a tricky business. All our efforts were at the mercy of the rain god (*Indra Devta*). Whenever the raid god was happy with us, we would get plenty of rain and, of course, a good harvest. But that was not always the case. I feel that my grandfather and his father lived precariously in this village. They inherited a sense of insecurity from their parents and passed it on to their children. I remember living with a feeling that we were poor and we did not have enough to eat. For years my family could only grow red pulses (*arhar*) because they can survive with little water. I have heard stories from my elders that for many days even the well-to-do families used to survive on bread (*roti*) and water (*pani*). At least in our life time we all have questioned the decision of our ancestors to continue to live in Shahargaon.

During this early period Shahargaon Jats also were politically dominated by nearby Jat villages having different regional affiliations and belonging to different lineages. These differences exaggerated inter-village conflict and competition for resources. Jats in other villages represented an ever present threat of physical violence, encroachment on landholdings, and competition in marketing. Unable to establish economic and marital alliances with Jat families in neighboring villages, Shahargaon Jats carried out such exchanges primarily with their parent village of Purgaon.

The interaction of Shahargaon Jats with the outside world was limited. Jat men only rarely visited the wholesale market in Mandi to trade their produce or to buy essential supplies. Although women worked in the fields, they could not leave the village unless accompanied by a male relative. Feeling threatened by their neighbors further reinforced the traditional son preference and seclusion of women as a means to protect against violence and ensure the survival of the community.

Historically, men and women in Shahargaon experienced unequal treatment, especially in regard to marriage, mobility, education, and employment. Shahargaon Jat families fit the general patriarchal pattern of North India. Sohan Lal explained:

> There were only a few men in the village. Our founding fathers were new arrivals in a strange distant land. They did not know how things worked in this new region. They were especially unsure of the intentions of the neighboring villagers toward them. The surrounding villages belonged to the Jats from different lineages and clans. Then there were other villages that belonged to non-Jat communities. Those periods must

have been scary times. I have heard of many incidents when fights broke out between Shahargaon Jats and the neighboring communities. Men were concerned about guarding their village boundary because the village boundaries were not clearly marked. So there was always disagreement over village boundaries between villages. Another concern at that time was attacks on our women by men from other villages. Because we were so few, our women had to work in the fields a lot. We needed their labor. This also made them vulnerable to attacks from other villagers. Men were always on guard against such attacks. I guess our past has made us what we are today. In those days we were untrusting of our neighbors and were paranoid about our women. Today were untrusting of this urban world and are worried about our girls.

In the middle of his introspective reflection, Sohan Lal paused to smoke his hookah, a traditional smoking pipe, and reminded me to check if the tape recorder was properly working. I assured him that I was recording his story. He continued:

So you tell me, what else we could do? We preferred sons because we needed men to defend our village and our women. We needed men to survive in this hostile environment. Men are more powerful than women and can wield sticks to defend their territory. Women cannot do that. In those days, we could not rely on police because this entire area was at quite a distance from the city limits. In fact, it was outside of the city. We lived in an isolated area. We were alone; there was no one to help us. We had to help ourselves. Women are vulnerable. Any attack on our women meant an attack on us, our prestige, and our way of life. We needed men; so we preferred sons.

Sohan Lal's comments rationalize his community's history of male dominance, but his apologetic tone reveals doubt about continuing to embrace gender inequality in the future. Achieving such awareness may be the first step in addressing the problem.

Women's Lives and Agricultural Roles in Pre-1970s Shahargaon

Jat women worked as agricultural laborers during the pre-1970s period. The small size of the Shahargaon population and poor land quality made labor a crucial resource problem. Since farming was the only reliable means to meet basic needs, Jat families employed labor intensive agricultural methods. Family survival necessitated that the women and children actively participate in agricultural production, both in the field and in post-harvest activities. Women performed almost all the work associated with threshing and winnowing, collecting fodder, caring for cattle, and processing cow dung into fuel cakes (Figure 2.5).

F I G U R E 2.5   Jat woman carrying firewood (© Sunil K. Khanna)

Despite these important economic roles performed by women, male informants in Shahargaon only rarely acknowledged their contribution (Figure 2.6). I learned about this aspect of village history from several women who talked about their own lives and those of their mothers-in-law in the pre-1970s period (Figure 2.7). They shared much of this information during several unstructured group interviews. I made little attempt to restrict the conversation and respected each woman's right to tell her story and express her opinions. From these interview sessions I also learned about marriage, women's seclusion and isolation, and pregnancy and childbirth.

Phoolwati, a Jat woman in her late sixties, indicated that life was harsh during the agricultural days. Jat women had to be tough to survive and to ensure the survival of their families and children:

> I was very young, maybe 16 years old, when I got married. I did not like
> living here. We did not have enough food here. Although I did not come
> from a rich family, growing up we had plenty of food. I used to cry a lot

F I G U R E 2.6   Jat woman carrying a packet of cow dung cakes (© Sunil K. Khanna)

and complained to my mother-in-law. We had to do a lot of work on our own. Men owned the fields and could tell women in the household anything they wanted us to do. They were the masters and we were their servants. We did not own anything. We neither owned land nor house-hold goods. Everything belonged to men. While men only worked in the fields, we had to perform all domestic chores, take care of the animals, feed our families, and then also help out in the fields. Of course, men expected us to help them in agricultural work. But we never expected them to help us with domestic work. After two years of my marriage, I got pregnant and my eldest daughter was born. By the time I was 35 or 40, I had a large

F I G U R E 2.7   Jat woman preparing a meal (© Sunil K. Khanna)

family of my own to take care of. I got pregnant six times and I have three sons and two daughters. I lost one daughter to some unknown illness. With the passage of time I felt more settled here in Shahargaon. I did visit my parents, but I always wanted to return back to this village. Life was hard here, but once I had my family the work here did not bother me. I did not think about my parents and now I am all settled here.

Darshna, a Jat woman in her mid-thirties, talked about the experiences of her mother-in-law:

My mother-in-law told me that when she came to this village she was only 15 years old. She missed her parents and sibling and wanted to go back home. She did not like this village. It was not like her birth village. She felt very isolated and powerless. Her relatives never visited in this village. It is not considered appropriate among our people to visit a daughter's home after her marriage. My mother-in-law could only visit her parents once a year and that too after undertaking a two-day long journey on a bullock-cart. For her it was especially difficult to adjust in this village because she came from a rich landowner's family. She got married into a family that had two small pieces of land. Her husband's family was poor. The land was arid and she had to work hard both at home and in the fields to eke out a living. Her mother-in-law and sisters-in-law also worked hard, so there was no reason for her to complain or to expect that she should be treated differently. Not much has changed for women in this village. While I am telling you the story of my mother-in-law, it is my story as well. The only difference is that, unlike my mother-in-law, I did not have to work in the fields. Families here had stopped farming when I got married and came to live with my husband's family.

The words of Phoolwati and Darshna describe their powerless lives and demanding productive roles in a time of severe economic hardship. Both women also mention a difficult period of adjustment after moving into the husband's family and a sense of isolation as a result of patrilocal residence.

Daughter Disfavor and Marriage in Pre-1970s Shahargaon

Shahargaon Jat women had closely-spaced pregnancies while continuing to participate in agricultural activities. Everyone considered a large family as vital to their survival, and they made no attempt to limit family size. Their goal was to maximize the number of sons. Jat elders recounted commonly used proverbs that underscore parental preference for sons and disfavor for daughters:

The number of sons is equal to the number of wooden sticks and the number of sticks determines the political and social prestige of a family and the land it can control (*Jitney bête utne lath, jitney lath utne izzat aur utna kabza*).

One can never have enough rain or sons (*Meenh aur bête jitney hun utney kum*).

Parents are unlucky if a son dies; but they are lucky if a daughter dies (*Beta mare badnaseeb ka; beti mare kushnaseeb ke*).

A daughter's father is considered weak and unfortunate (*Beti ka baap kamzor aur badnaseeb hove hai*).

Jat parents acted upon their disfavor of daughters by reducing their allocations of household resources or demanding more of them in performing domestic and farm labor. They rationalized poor treatment of daughters by saying that "raising a daughter is equivalent to caring for a tree that will bear fruits for someone else" or "a daughter is like a bottomless well that only drains a family's resources." Jat parents also feared that a young unmarried daughter would be easy prey for men from neighboring villagers and that having her in their home as a target for sexual predation created a risk to the family's social honor. They tried to reduce this risk by severely restricted a daughter's movement.

Unreliable agricultural yields, poverty, distance from traditional marital villages in Haryana, and the practice of village and regional exogamy made it difficult to forge marital alliances. Haryana Jats traditionally practiced clan, village, and regional exogamy in arranging marital alliances. Ideally, clan exogamy extended to the father, mother, paternal grandmother, and maternal grandmother. Residence after marriage was patrilocal and the inheritance of property was patrilineal. Although the ideal marital alliance for Shahargaon Jats after migration continued to be with their traditional marital villages in Haryana, most Jat families from prosperous villages in Haryana refused to establish marital alliances with them. Relatively wealthy Haryana Jats regarded Shahargaon Jats as "hilly" (*pahari*), and joked about their poverty and low social status. They derogatorily called Shahargaon a "hilly village" (*pahari gaon*) and its women "hilly Jat women" (*pahari jatni or paharo*), who could be persuaded to marry in exchange for as little as a "bullock cart of hay" (*bhuse ka thela*).

The term "hilly" (*pahari*) in addition to describing the hilly terrain in Shahargaon, also invokes a set of ideas and beliefs associated with north Indian communities that do not follow the upper-caste prescriptive codes for establishing marital alliances (Berreman 1972). Hilly communities exhibit distinctive social characteristics such as polyandry (a woman having more than one husband), divorce by mutual consent, remarriage of widows and divorcees, and the acceptance of inter-caste marriages. Affluent North Indian Hindu communities believe that these social characteristics and associated practices are unusual and objectionable. By using the term "hilly" Haryana Jats labeled Shahargaon Jats as having low social status (Khanna 2001). Recalling the hardships faced by Shahargaon Jats during the early settlement period, Dalbir Singh, a middle-aged Jat shopkeeper, narrated the following story to illustrate the discriminatory and mocking attitude of Haryana Jats:

A Shahargaon Jat once visited his distant wealthy relative in Haryana. The host family offered him sugarcane juice. The guest liked the drink and since he had never tasted sugarcane juice he kept asking for more. Upon his return to Shahargaon he boasted about his experience of drinking the sweet sugarcane juice. His friends requested a taste of his sweet spit, but he refused the offer. Instead, he decided to spit in the village well so that the entire Shahargaon community could taste and enjoy the sweetness of the sugarcane juice.

Sugarcane is a profitable cash crop usually grown in the fertile Indo-Gangetic plains of north India. In Haryana, only affluent Jat communities can afford to grow it. Domestic production and consumption of sugarcane juice is a symbol of high social and economic status among the Jats. During the pre-1970s period, the inability of Shahargaon to grow sugarcane served to reinforce their low status in the minds of affluent Haryana Jats.

Traditionally, among the Jats marriage involves a transfer of goods in the form of dowry from the bride's family to the groom's family. The Jats also offered payments of cash or goods to obtain brides from poor families. These practices were especially common in economically struggling Jat communities. As Chowdhry explains:

> The important role played by women in the economy also led to wide acceptance of the prevalent custom of sale and purchase of brides among the economically distressed peasantry. In the 19th century, except among a few better-off families, this custom was observed to have been universal not only among the Jats but also among the agricultural and lower castes. (Chowdhry 1994:65-66)

In the Indian context, a dowry is a collection of gifts given to a daughter by her parents and other natal relatives at the time of her wedding. These gifts usually involve household goods, jewelry, clothes, and cash. The amount of dowry given to a daughter is a primary indicator of the economic and social status of her natal family and a secondary indicator of the economic and social status of her husband's family. Jat parents usually provide a substantial dowry to ensure that their own daughters "married up" in social and economic status. In keeping with the practices common to the Jat community, Shahargaon Jats offered lucrative dowries to seek hypergamous alliances (meaning to "marry up") for their daughters and to establish a position of respect and honor among neighboring Jat communities. Elders estimated the expense associated with dowry to be at least equal to the annual income of a family. In some cases, Jat parents were forced to borrow money from their relatives or moneylenders in other villages to pay for the daughter's dowry. According to Sohan Lal:

> Even in the days when families in Shahargaon were poor, Jat parents never relented from spending money on dowry. Given their meager family income they could not afford to give a large dowry. But they did so by borrowing money from relatives or accepting loans at high interest

rates. Sometimes they even sold their animals, gold, or other assets to pay for dowry. Shahargaon daughters were married the same way Haryana girls were married. They received household utensils, bedcovers, gold jewelry, clothes, and other household items as gifts from their parents. Some of these items were specifically meant for the groom and his family members. Regardless of their poor economic status, early Shahargaon settlers pretended to be affluent and resourceful Jats at the time of the wedding of their daughters.

During the pre–1970s period, Jat girls married at an early age, sometimes as early as 13 years old. Parents negotiated marital alliances with the help of the village barber who assisted in finding a suitable match and in finalizing the timing, exchange of gifts, and other important details. An elaborate religious ceremony marked the passage of the first of two stages of marriage. Following the ceremony the bride stayed at her natal home. The term *liviayo* (literally, to bring) refers to the time when the bridegroom and his relatives come to take the bride to her affinal village. This change of residence and consummation of the marriage (*gauna*) took place one or two years later. On both occasions the bride's family arranged a feast for the marriage party and provided gifts for the groom's relatives.

Shahargaon Jats paid dowries and spent large sums of money in arranging their daughters' marriages even though in those days daughters worked in the fields and were economic assets. The marriage of a daughter meant the loss of an economically productive member in the household. Brides marrying Jat men in Shahargaon were expected to quickly take on the responsibility of doing household chores. They were also considered by the community as productive agricultural laborers vital to the prosperity of a family. The low economic status and the struggling nature of the Shahargaon community made it difficult for the Jat men to obtain brides from affluent Haryana Jat families. Since the productive and reproductive roles of women were seen as necessary for the survival of the Shahargaon community, Jat men grew increasingly desperate for brides.

During the early settlement period, the limited availability of Jat brides from Haryana led to the practice of fraternal polyandry where two brothers would share a wife. Elders also recalled instances in which the shortage of willing brides led Jat men to marry non-Jat women or to secure a marriage by threat of force. They described these types of alliances as "low prestige" marriages and suggested that fraternal polyandrous households and marriages by force were common during the early settlement period. The elders did not identify the specific families involved in these low prestige marriages to avoid embarrassing their descendents who still live in the village. Om Prakash discussed inter-caste marriages while being careful to maintain confidentiality:

In those days we were poor and we felt abandoned by our parent community in Haryana. Our poverty was perhaps the biggest cause of this abandonment. Our poverty also made us vulnerable to threats from our neighboring communities. We had to find a way to keep surviving. One way we could ensure our survival was by having as many sons as possible and for that we needed wives. Many of our men could not find Jat women from Haryana, and ended up bringing in non-Jat women and then marrying them here in the village. These women first were brought to the village to work in the fields. Later, Jat men married them. I know of one such case where a woman from the potter (*Kumhar*) caste came to the village and a Jat man married her.

He justified the instances of polyandry and marriage with non-Jat women by pointing out the advantages of ensuring the continuity of the family, protecting the lineage, preserving control over land ownership, and exploiting the productive and reproductive roles of women.

Shahargaon Jats practiced widow remarriage, in a sense reclaiming women, sometimes by a ritual called *karewa* or *chaddar andazi*, in which a man throws a white sheet (*chaddar*) over the widow's head, signifying his acceptance of her as his wife. Shahargaon Jats describe such levirate marriages as "wearing bangles" (*chura pahenana*), a ritual act granting social consent for cohabitation between a widow and her husband's younger brother. During the ritual the prospective husband places glass bangles on the widow's wrist in the presence of a group of relatives and neighbors. During the early settlement period, the practices of *karewa* and polyandry co-existed in Shahargaon. In some cases, *karewa* alliances were merely symbolic (unconsummated) as a means of protecting the extended family's property rights and avoiding sexual indiscretion on part of the widow. Although Shahargaon Jats occasionally accepted brides from non-Jat castes and were flexible in dealing with traditional marriage rules, they always married their daughters back into the Haryana Jat villages located in rural districts surrounding Delhi particularly in the districts of Sonipat, Panipat, Rohtak, and Jhajjar (Figure 2.8).

Because Shahargaon Jats were poorer than their Haryana counterparts, most Shahargaon families could not achieve the ideal of hypergamy by providing an adequate dowry and could not marry their daughters into wealthier Jat families in Haryana. Jat elders reported that late marriages were common for Shahargaon daughters, and that some unmarried women stayed to live in the village. Families kept their daughters at home because they could not meet the dowry demands for a hypergamous alliance and refused the dishonor of accepting a less desirable marriage proposal. These families faced social condemnation for being greedy by exploiting unmarried older daughters as agricultural and domestic laborers. During the early settlement period, intra-village conflict often arose as a result of the alleged or actual sexual indiscretions of unmarried daughters who then occasionally resorted to suicide.

The practices of fraternal polyandry, marriage by force, widow remarriage, marriage with non-Jat families, and delayed marriages all represent means by which Shahargaon Jats ensured their survival. Their circumstances during the early settlement period of Shahargaon were defined primarily by poverty, isolation, and physical insecurity. According to several Jat elders, Shahargaon families chose these

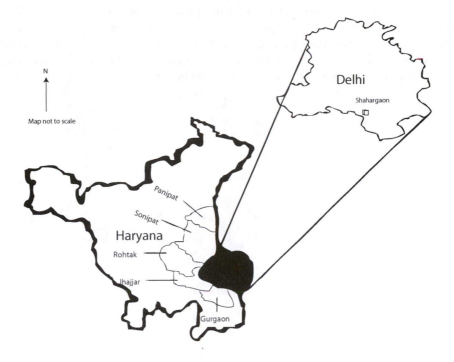

F I G U R E 2.8   Map showing the location of Shahargaon's preferred marriage districts in Haryana (© Sunil K. Khanna)

desperate means of survival only when they had no other choice. They were reluctant to identify the families that engaged undesirable marriage practices to save embarrassment, because at present they still consider these practices as unbecoming of a true Jat way of life. In the last three decades, the economic status of Jat families has significantly improved and the community as a whole is protective of its traditional Jat identity. Under these circumstances, any link to a controversial past can negatively influence their image among Haryana Jats and affect their ability to make future marital arrangements.

HISTORICAL LEGACY

For the Shahargaon Jats, traditions and practices associated with their agricultural way of life during the pre-1970s period not only defined their peasant identity, but also served as a lens for viewing the outside world in the post-1970s period. Their stories and experiences establish boundaries separating rural Shahargaon from its urban context. The patriarchal context of their culture, kinship and marriage rules, and the struggle for survival in a hostile world created circumstances that exacerbated gender inequality by forcing the Jat community to impose restrictions on women's mobility and education. Their very survival depended on exploiting women not only as producers but also as reproducers. Later in the post–1970s period these historical patterns of gender inequality also played a major role in structuring Shahargaon's relationship with the urban world of New Delhi.

Chapter 3

✳

Urban Transformation:
The Post-1970s Period

This chapter focuses on changes experienced and narrated by Shahargaon's Jat residents, as they have taken place since the village became a part of the "urban agglomeration" of New Delhi (the post-1970s period). For more than two centuries after founding of the village, Jat families practiced and preserved their traditional peasant way of life. Now thirty-five years after Shahargaon's urban assimilation, agricultural work has all but died, yet traditions associated with the peasant lifestyle continue to define and shape the community's perception of itself and its interaction with emergent consumerism in the urban world.

FROM VILLAGE TO "URBAN AGGLOMERATION"

During my fieldwork in 2003, I noticed that the ongoing construction of new houses, shops, and the addition of new rooms and floors to the old village homes had given Shahargaon the appearance of a hodgepodge agglomeration of fully and partially built houses (Figure 3.1).

The unplanned vertical and horizontal expansion of houses for living space and commerce has made the village lanes uncomfortably narrow and dark. The entire village area appeared as a mesh of crisscrossing narrow lanes further branching into even narrower alleys (*raste*) (Figure 3.2, page 37).

Each alley was flanked on both sides by brick houses (*pukka*). Young men in the village looked and behaved more like residents of New Delhi (*Delhites*) than as inhabitants of a small village (Figure 3.3, page 38).

They wore locally made shoes imitating such brand names as Nike, Reebok, and Adidas, and T-shirts with imprints of American sports celebrities and Hollywood stars. In casual conversations they bragged about the special features of their new cellular phones and Walkman recorders, and responded to my questions

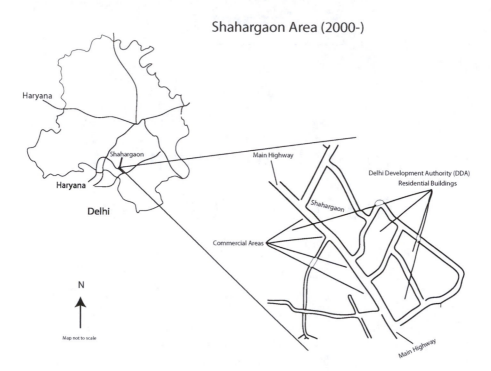

FIGURE 3.1   Shahargaon area in recent years (© Sunil K. Khanna)

posed in Hindi with intentional use of the English language. By all appearances, everyday life in Shahargaon appeared inextricably connected with the surrounding city of New Delhi.

From Isolation to Assimilation

In stark contrast to its past as an isolated villages, Shahargaon is now part of one of New Delhi's fastest growing urban markets and residential neighborhoods. This change was brought about by a series of state-sponsored policies aimed at transforming the villages surrounding New Delhi into urban neighborhoods. In 1972, the Delhi Development Authority (DDA)—the regional development authority— acquired the agricultural land surrounding Shahargaon to accommodate the urban expansion. The Delhi Development Authority labeled Shahargaon and other villages suffering the same fate as rural blocks to be collectively transformed into urban neighborhoods with newly built residential and commercial complexes. Shahargaon Jat families received compensation money equivalent to the value of their land as assessed jointly by the Delhi Development Authority and the Office of the Land Commissioner of New Delhi. Eventually by the late 1970s, Shahargaon Jats abandoned farming and either sought employment in New Delhi or started small-scale businesses. Assimilation into New Delhi necessitated that Jat families start buying food and other consumable goods in the urban market. The sudden loss of agricultural land at first exposed villagers to considerable financial hardship, as no programs were in place to ensure a smooth transition toward

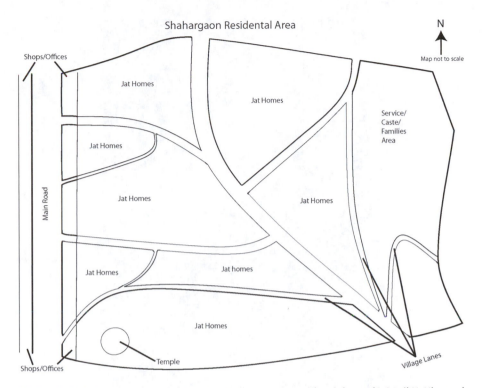

FIGURE 3.2   Line diagram showing Shahargaon's residential area (© Sunil K. Khanna)

non-farm means of earning an income. Sohan Lal commented that the agricultural way of life was still more difficult:

> As farmers, we lived more or less hand-to-mouth. What we used to grow was barely sufficient for our own survival. A good crop would improve things as we could sell our surplus produce in Mandi and make some profit. Our lives changed when DDA came into Shahargaon. It improved a little bit, but it has been hard for us as a community to adapt to this new urban world. Some of us became rich overnight while others remained poor; some families had more food than others. All of us could not become urbanized (*shahri*) at the same time. We felt divided and intimidated by this new world that was forced upon us by the DDA. Dalbir, a middle-aged Jat man, echoed Sohan Lal's views in the following words: When the DDA came to this village, everything changed. Our land was taken away from us and we were forced to live in this small residential section. The walls around us grew taller and we lost sight of our fields. We only knew how to be farmers. We did not know how to earn a livelihood by any other means. Some families in the village rented portions of their homes to outsiders just to have a steady source of income. Others started looking for jobs on construction projects

FIGURE 3.3   A narrow alleyway in Shahargaon (© Sunil K. Khanna)

that were going on around the village. It was heartbreaking to work as cheap labor on buildings that the DDA was constructing on our land. We were no longer masters of our destiny. Instead, we became slaves of the DDA.

During the 1980s, the Delhi Development Authority opened up a large residential colony and two shopping centers on Shahargaon's agricultural land. As a result of urban development, real estate values in the village and its adjoining areas increased greatly. Many Jat families have taken advantage the new housing market by selling and renting portions of their residential property. These changes have quickly transformed Shahargaon from an isolated and impoverished village into a region of intense commercial activity and a strategic area of economic growth. Families have built additional floors and lofts on top of the old village homes (Figure 3.4). Renting space for residential and commercial purposes has become one of the major sources of income for Jat families.

Shahargaon's strategic location and proximity to major centers of commerce make it attractive for a number of businesses, such as car showrooms and export

FIGURE 3.4   A house under construction alongside a narrow unpaved lane in Shahargaon (© Sunil K. Khanna)

companies, to rent commercial space. Commercial rent in Shahargaon is cheaper than in the adjacent older neighborhood of New Delhi because government building codes and regulations are not often enforced. In the villages surrounding New Delhi, including Shahargaon, the distinction between rural and urban areas is demarcated by "Red Thread" (*Lal Dora*). "Red Thread" zoning originated as part of land tenure and revenue policies during the British colonial period. The area bounded by "Red Thread" is "village land" protected from the authority of the urban government. According to a notification sent by the New Delhi Administration in 1963, residents of Shahargaon did not require government permits or permission for constructing a house or adding to an existing house. As a result, Shahargaon residents constructed buildings and added floors to existing buildings without any objections from the Municipal Corporation of Delhi (MCD) or the regulatory office of the Delhi Development Authority. In response to rampant construction of buildings in "Red Thread" zones in villages bordering New Delhi, the High Court of New Delhi in 1984 rescinded the earlier notification and ruled that villagers must obtain proper permission before constructing new houses or additions to existing buildings. Despite this ruling, the implementation of laws regulating illegal construction has been lax.

One of the most visible and dramatic aspects of social change in Shahargaon is the rapid transformation of the village architecture (Figure 3.5). Old village houses, uneven house constructions, and additions to existing structures now

FIGURE 3.5   A section of Shahargaon's commercial area (© Sunil K. Khanna)

define this small area in the middle of a bustling urban business center. Yet Shahargaon retains its rural ambience where narrow lanes and dark alleys demarcate the village space from the outside world.

A few old village homes have been demolished to build new taller and more efficient structures. Some of the old structures were not demolished, and now are submerged under new construction on the top of the old (Figure 3.6). This visible and dramatic aspect of architectural change in the village is an appropriate metaphor

FIGURE 3.6   An old village house (© Sunil K. Khanna)

FIGURE 3.7   A new village house (© Sunil K. Khanna)

for cultural transformation. Perhaps the old is giving way to the new, or resisting the new, or both (Figure 3.7).

In the mid–1980s, a handful of Jat families started catering to the urban market by opening retail stores selling construction materials, tea stalls/road side eateries (*dhabas*), and real estate. Gradually, Internet cafes, clothing stores, and fast-food restaurants began to proliferate in the same area. Since 2003, this urban market has attracted the best quality retail stores, video game parlors, and fancy restaurants. The surrounding residential colony established by the Delhi Development Authority provides a rich clientele for small-scale commercial opportunities in Shahargaon. Everyday interaction in the market superimposes an urban context on the rural character of the village.

THE RICH AND THE POOR

According to my 2003 household survey, Shahargaon's total population is 1336, distributed among 245 households. The Jat community forms the largest social group (70.2 percent). Increased urban contact has improved the overall economic status of Jat families; they live in houses built with bricks and cement (*pukka ghar*) equipped with electricity and water connections. In order to assess the economic status of Jat households, I used information pertaining to household composition, land and property ownership, occupation, household income, education, and household appliances. The confiscation of agricultural land by the state made land ownership an unreliable criterion. However, retrospective information on land ownership provided an indication of change in economic status. I grouped 179 Jat households in Shahargaon into the following three economic categories:

Group A comprises "affluent" households (51 households or 29 percent) who were successfully able to invest the compensation money given by the Delhi Development Authority into a business such as a small-scale industry or a shop (Figure 3.8). Before land confiscation, the bigger family units represented among these households owned large pieces of agricultural land for which they later

F I G U R E 3.8   Jat couple from *Group A* (© Sunil K. Khanna)

received substantial sums of compensation money. Some households in this group had more than one source of income, as men were employed either in the military or government service. Most members of affluent households, including women and children, were formally educated. Sons typically studied in expensive private English-medium schools, whereas daughters were most likely to continue their education at less expensive Hindi-medium schools located within walking distance from the village. Two women belonging to different households in this group were employed, both as school teachers. Adults in this economic group were well informed about the available health care services and could afford private health care. Most households had at least one television set, a cooking gas connection, a car, a scooter or motorcycle, and other electric appliances. These households belong to the Upper Income Group (monthly income $2000 or more).

Group B (97 households or 54 percent) includes families who did not successfully invest their compensation money but still received extra income from renting a small portion of their residential property to entrepreneurs for commercial purpose. In some households, men held low paying jobs as drivers or security guards. A few men had been educated at the high school level, but women typically had not studied beyond primary school. Most sons and daughters studied at less expensive Hindi-medium schools. In some households, however, sons studied in private English-medium schools. Families tended to use government-sponsored health care and sought private health care only in case of an emergency. Most families owned a television set, a cooking gas connection, and a bicycle (Figure 3.9). These households belong to the Middle Income Group (monthly income from $1000 to $2000).

Group C (31 households or 17 percent) includes families who could or did not successfully invest their compensation money. They lived in houses in the interior of the village, a location of little commercial value. A Jat man in this group commented, "We are living in a state that can be described as hand-to-mouth." Most households in Group C did not have any source of regular income. Men worked either as part-time laborers or on small contract jobs related to construction. A few men also worked as real estate brokers to earn extra income. Most men and women were educated only at the primary school level. Parents said they wanted to educate their children, especially

F I G U R E 3.9   Mother and children from *Group B* (© Sunil K. Khanna)

girls, up to the middle-school level available in the government run village school. However, they sent their boys to government run high schools located in neighboring areas. They uniformly sought health care from government run clinics and hospitals. Most households in this group did not have cooking gas connections and could not afford vehicles or luxury household items such as television sets (Figure 3.10). These households belong to the Low Income Group (monthly income less than $1000).

F I G U R E 3.10   Jat couple from *Group C* (© Sunil K. Khanna)

Participation in the urban economy pushes relatively affluent Shahargaon Jats (Groups A and B) to redefine their identity from that of rural (*dehati*) peasants to that of urbanized (*shahri*) residents of New Delhi. They use their recently improved economic status to align themselves with the educated, affluent, and modern society of New Delhi. They interact with people from the immigrant residential settlement on a daily basis—people whom they label as "urban" (*shahri*). In their interaction with urbanites, these Jats attempt to show-off by using English words in casual conversation; by seeking treatment from an expensive allopathic specialist; and by sending sons to private English-medium schools. In contrast, less economically-successful Jat families (Group C) tend to exaggerate their agricultural identity and idealize cultural practices associated with a traditional agricultural way of life. They maintain a boundary between themselves as Jats and the surrounding multiethnic urban population, expressing a sense of nostalgia for an idealized version of their life in rural and insular Shahargaon.

THE CONFLICT WITHIN

As discussed in the previous chapter, Shahargaon's agricultural past and a peasant way of life collectively exert a strong influence on the community today. Jat families are better off than they were when Shahargaon was an isolated village. Yet some members of the community feel that the urban contact has created more conflict and discontent than prosperity. Differences in adapting to a new way of life have led to considerable inequality in household income and the inability of some families to take advantage of the growing urban market. Even members of more affluent Jat families (Groups A and B) express a sense of financial insecurity because they are not sure how long their businesses will be able to compete and remain viable in the urban world. Sohan Lal expressed his concerns:

> As new and fancy stores enter our market, the competition will increase and our livelihood will be at risk. We have specialty clothing stores that are taking over that business in the market. These stores are owned by rich families that own many other stores in New Delhi. In order to attract rich and educated clients from the nearby DDA residential colony, these stores employ staff that can speak English. Jat businessmen here cannot compete with that; they do not know English and they do not have a lot of money to hire trained English-speaking staff from improving their business.

Several fast-food restaurants, including Pizza Hut, Dominos, and Burger King, have already entered the Shahargaon market taking a big share of business away from the locally-owned eateries (*dhabas*). For many Shahargaon residents it is becoming increasingly difficult to compete with these well-financed business ventures. Therefore, in spite of improvement in annual household income, many

Jat store owners do not feel a sense of financial security and are ambivalent about the long-term consequences of urban assimilation.

Differences in class status within the village have significantly influenced people's opinions and given rise to conflict. I heard complaints about the income gap between the rich and poor families. Conflicting opinions are most evident in discussions where the village residents gather to play cards or chess. The conflict often occurs between disgruntled old-timers who complain about the congested traffic in village lanes and educated urbanites influenced by mass media who regard the New Delhi lifestyle as efficient and fashionable, compared to the village which is inefficient and old-fashioned.

Chote Ram, a Jat man in his seventies born in Shahargaon and a life-long resident of the village, expressed his concern about the loss of traditions and customs:

> I am a proud Jat peasant and despite all that is happening around this village, it will always be a village of peasants. All this change is the fault of our government. It came and took our land. They promised us many things. They told us that life would be better than what it was at that time. They promised they would give us the money, which they did. We did not have any say in the value of our land. Based upon the amount of land each family owned, we were given compensation money at the lowest possible rate. With that money, only a few families have been successful in adapting to the urban life.

Like other Jat families in Shahargaon, Chote Ram's family practiced agriculture. "We farmed well into the early 1970s," he recalled:

> From the day I could remember, my father and uncles would plow the fields and work there all day long. We were one of the richest families in the village, but we did not think of ourselves as different or special in the village. We just wanted to be part of the village community. We would grow food in quantities to feed our family and to sell in the wholesale market. It was sufficient and we lived a life that was oriented to the bottom line attitude. Now the attitude has changed. We no longer think about the bottom line.

For some Jat families, compensation money proved to be of little help. Dalbir, a Jat man in his late fifties, commented:

> Everyone liked receiving the compensation money. But only a few of us knew what to do with it. Most believed that it was free money and they could do anything with it. We were farmers then and getting large amounts of cash was not something people were used to in the village. We did not know what to do with the DDA money. Naturally, it was wasted on gambling and alcohol.

Om Prakash's family is one of the success stories. His family was able to successfully invest compensation money into opening a small construction materials business. He told me that his family quickly realized that they had to move toward a new way of life. He continued:

> Early in the transition period, the Shahargaon marketplace was small. But we were patient, we did not panic. We learned that the government was going to build a residential colony on our land. So we knew there will be a need for construction materials and saw the business potential of a construction materials shop. We wanted to take advantage of a growing market and we did well.

Om Prakash's family is presently active in the Shahargaon Jat community in sponsoring local festivals and community events especially those associated with raising awareness of the value of education for daughters and need for equality among boys and girls. But this family is one of only a handful that can afford to be charitable. For most Jat families, the transition to urban economy has been problematic. They feel a sense of alienation not only from the government but also from fellow members of the Jat community.

Kishan Chand, a man in his sixties, worked as a security guard in a nearby factory. Relying on limited income, his family was barely managing to survive. In 2001, he borrowed money from a friend to construct an unauthorized extra room on the roof of his house. He has benefited financially from renting out the room, but is afraid that the Delhi Development Authority may disallow the new construction and demolish it. When I asked him about the support he received from the Delhi Development Authority, he became contemplative and a bit confused. "Do you think the government or the Delhi Development Authority is for people like me?" he asked. Then he added:

> The DDA is not for us poor people in the village; it is for the rich. I have no expectations from the Delhi Development Authority, and all I want is for it to stay as far away from me as possible. I am not angry toward the government; it is just that it has no role in my life. I live in my house in the village and we are protected because we live within the residential area of our village; in our "Red Thread" (*Lal Dora*) area. I am angry toward my neighbors who, now that they have become rich, have forgotten us and are behaving like urbanites (*shahris*). Unlike in the past, sharing our problems and resources is not something we do anymore.

> Ram, a middle-aged Jat shop owner in Shahargaon, also commented:Shahargaon is not a village anymore. It is a city or at least a part of New Delhi. Of course, our quality of life has improved. We have cars, television sets, and everything else, but our village has not become an attractive place to live. Instead, it has turned into a congested inner city ghetto. We now have serious problems of alcoholism, gambling, social

conflict, and disobedience among children. Men are busy earning money. They prefer to spend their evenings with friends drinking alcohol and gambling rather than spend time at home. Children are not interested in studying. They disobey their elders all the time. This village and its people have become blind followers of the modern people of New Delhi.

A strong sense exists among such families that they are not part of the urban center and have been completely left behind. In the past when the village had an agricultural base families cooperated with each other. Individuals now struggle for survival alone in a consumer-driven world with little sense of cooperation or collective responsibility.

INTENSIFICATION OF GENDER INEQUALITY

In the preceding chapter, I discussed how the relationship between men and women and women's roles in pre-1970s Shahargaon closely reflected the norms associated with their peasant culture. The Shahargaon Jat community historically consisted of paternal joint family households in which men held decision-making power—a characteristic common to many patriarchal landowning peasant communities in north India. Men related by patrilineal kinship share the power, and women who are not related to each other and marry into the village from elsewhere have access to power only through men. Although every patriarchal society is unique in certain aspects, all such societies tend to share a set of common characteristics—a preference for having sons over daughters, limited or no property rights for women, and restrictions on women's mobility in public. Shahargaon's social structure fits this pattern, but is now undergoing change due to urban contact.

Urban assimilation has differently impacted the lives of men and women in the village. Examining this issue is crucial to understanding why son preference, a characteristic of the Jat peasant society, continues to persist. During a group interview, Kaushalya, Janki, and Rajbala—three Jat women in their late fifties—talked with me about how urban contact has impacted the lives of men and women in urbanizing Shahargaon:

KAUSHALYA: Shahargaon is now an affluent village and its families are rich. But money has made us more rural than before when we were poor. Shahargaon families own color televisions, stereos, and even have big homes. Men in the village now own and drive latest model cars, but women cannot leave their homes alone and girls cannot study beyond the village school. Boys attend English-medium private schools in New Delhi, but girls go to Hindi-medium government schools. Parents want their sons to be educated, but do not show the same concern for their daughters. Women are taught to focus on domestic work and family life. We were told that the new ways are going to be better for all of us. But here in Shahargaon, only men have become urban. Women have not.

> Women are still rural in this village. Half of Shahargaon has rural people (*dehati*) living in a city (*shahar*).

JANKI: We thought that life in the city would offer new things and we all will be safe and rich. I did not like working on the farm, but I hate not having anything at all. All day long we just work inside the house or sit here and talk.

RAJBALA: We are told to accept whatever our husbands tell us. We are told to do whatever our husbands ask us to do. We are treated as if we are dependent on our husbands for everything. When we worked in the fields, we were treated as working members of the family and we had some say in household decisions. Now, we have no say. We are now dependent on our husbands who are the decision makers in the family. We have no public life, we only have this life.

The benefits of urbanization do not accrue equally to men and women. Jat women's dreams of a new life have been shackled by the newly imposed restraints. As members of a traditionally patriarchal society, Shahargaon Jat women now feel less independent because their work roles were valued when the village had an agricultural way of life. In the new urban economy, men's roles as exclusive providers in generating income for the family through the urban market have conferred upon them a greater sense of power. Women's roles are limited to domestic duties which are devalued in the urban context, thus making them more dependent on men. Women have become even more secluded within the household and marginalized in the community than they were in the past.

Son preference appears to be intensifying in Shahargaon. Sons have become greater economic and political assets, adding to the strength and prestige of the family, whereas daughters are viewed as economic liabilities and social burdens whose morality must be protected. Jat parents rely on their sons to manage businesses and real estate ventures and to negotiate their relationships with the surrounding urban society. Although sons are no longer needed as agricultural laborers or as a defense force against physical violence perpetrated by nearby villages, a Jat family with no sons is still perceived as economically and politically weak. Jat parents perceive sons as able to take advantage of the economic opportunities available in the urban market and to ensure their survival and that of the community.

URBAN MEN AND RURAL WOMEN

Several studies have examined Indian women's marginal status under systems of patriarchy and the impact of social and economic changes on their lives (Harlan and Courtright 1995; Vallianatos 2006; Wadley 1994). These studies identify several factors, including urban contact, education, and occupation, that shape women's identity in the social context of patriarchy. Using ethnographic data, these studies demonstrate that increasing modernization and urban contact does not necessarily improve women's status or reduce son preference. They discredit the notion that increased urban contact will eventually alleviate the problems faced by women and recommend focusing on the ways in which hierarchical gender relations influence education and employment opportunities for women inside and outside the home.

Protecting Women and Family Prestige

The socioeconomic vulnerability of women is rooted in the dominant social ideology of patriarchy and is further exacerbated by women's exclusion from participation in the urban world. Opportunities have expanded in the urban market, but only for Jat men. Men deny women access to the same urban market because they fear the influence of a corrupt and dangerous urban world. Jat women rarely work outside the home to avoid encountering men regarded as "untrustworthy outsiders." Jat men feel that by allowing women to work outside the village, they are not only risking women's safety but also compromising their reputation as "peasant Jats from Haryana" (*Haryanavi Jat*). Restrictions placed on women are a sign of upward mobility and the prestige of the household. Families that allowed women to manage shops in Shahargaon during the early transition period drew scorn as the ones that "make their women work" (*aurton se dhanda karwate hain*). The term *dhanda* (literally, "work"), when used in this context, labels a working woman as a prostitute. Furthermore, a Jat husband who listens to his wife and consults her in economic matters incurs the stigma of being his "wife's servant" (*lugai ka naukar*). Women cannot leave the village without being accompanied by a male family member, further reducing their chances of gaining facility with the urban environment. Women complain about the limitations imposed on their mobility outside the village and express frustration over their life of confinement and boredom in performing repetitive domestic chores.

THE CUSTOM OF WEARING THE VEIL (*PURDAH*)

Jats expect women to cover their faces while moving outside of the home or interacting with non-family members, especially men. Wadley (1994), in her study of Karimpur—a multi-caste village in north India, suggests that the custom of wearing the veil (*purdah*) serves as a means to control women's activities and movements both within and outside the household and to reinforce social status of families in the community.

> Women should not be seen by strange men, nor should they talk to them. Unmarried girls are also restricted in their mobility, perhaps visiting the village shop for some spices or supplies for a festival, but always accompanied by other children. When a woman, especially a daughter-in-law, leaves her house she is covered in a shawl, and her sari pulled down to cover her face. Even in her courtyard, the end of her sari covers her face, and she speaks in a whisper in the presence of her husband and any male senior to him. She will also veil herself to show respect when other women are present or on ritual occasions (Wadley 1994: 52–53).

In urbanizing Shahargaon, the custom of the veil (*purdah*) requires that a woman covers her head and face when leaving home or in the presence of men (Figure 3.11). Families enforce such restrictions both within and outside of homes and confine the movement of women to so-called "safe zones" within the village. At present, only inner village lanes are safe zones for Jat women. Typically, a Jat woman can remove her veil only when she is inside her home or is in the presence of family members. This custom serves as a means for men to control women, as it forbids women from interacting with the outside world and excludes them from participating in economic activities outside the home (Figure 3.12).

Contrary to the notion that urbanization and improved class status will eventually reduce restrictions imposed by the veil, Jat women have become even more restricted and secluded. Dhanwati, a 33-year-old Jat woman stated:

Before marriage I lived in Bahardurgarh, District Rohtak, Haryana. I came to this village almost fifteen years ago. I studied up to Class XII and then my parents decided to arrange my marriage. They did not want to

F I G U R E   3.11   A Jat woman wearing a veil (© Sunil K. Khanna)

F I G U R E 3.12   A Jat mother-in-law wearing a veil (© Sunil K. Khanna)

send me to college. But my parents did not stop us from playing or going to markets (*bazaars*) with friends. I did not wear a veil until I got married. I did not mind hiding my face in front of my husband's brother or my father-in-law. But I don't like to cover my head and face when I go out to the market on the main street. My mother-in-law reminds me to cover my face when I walk my daughter to her school. I just don't like it, but I don't want my husband to get angry because he loves his mother very much. He tells me that we have two servants at home. So I should send them outside for household chores and for taking my daughter to school. My husband does not want me to work because he says I can have anything I want. But I want to take my daughter to school; I want to go out and see what is happening out there. My husband and I quarrel about this all the time.

Jat women complained that they will never learn how to live outside Shahargaon and will never be able to teach the ways of the urban world to their children, especially their daughters. Jat women and their talents continue to be devalued, as the new urban-capitalist economy in Shahargaon has reinforced traditional patriarchal ideology and narrowed women's roles to carriers of tradition and a means of maintaining customs and practices associated with the community's agrarian past. Women now represent an economically marginalized and spatially segregated underclass in Shahargaon.

EDUCATION, IDENTITY, AND MARRIAGE

Before Shahargaon's assimilation into the urban environment of New Delhi, it had only one primary school. The nearest secondary school was located in the nearby town of Mandi. Only a few boys and no girls attended the secondary school (Figure 3.13). After completion of the Delhi Development Authority housing project, three English-medium secondary schools and several preparatory and middle schools opened in the new residential settlement.

I documented a relatively large number of literate men and women in the community. According to my 2003 household survey, 69 percent of Jat men and 55 percent of Jat women are literate. In the context of a high value place on educational attainment, illiterate Jat men were embarrassed to admit to their poor education and blamed it on the lack of schools available during the pre-1970s

F I G U R E   3.13   A class in session in the village school (© Sunil K. Khanna)

period. Most illiterate Jat women blamed strict Jat tradition for their lack of education. The most revealing statistic is that only 23 percent of the girls under 19 are literate, compared to 57 percent of the boys in the same age group. Thus literacy for girls appears to be declining. Girls are not studying beyond the village school despite the availability of new educational opportunities in the nearby immigrant residential settlement.

A majority of Shahargaon Jat parents believe that education is important and want their children to attend school. They associate education with an overall successful life and improvement in economic status. Most believe that their children must have an education to cope with the new urban world. However, some feared that attending school would expose them to the "evils of urban society." They expressed concerns that English-medium schools would introduce their children to drugs, teach them not to respect the wishes of their parents, and encourage them to run away and seeking a "love marriage."

Most parents regarded English-medium education for their sons as crucial to the success of their families in the new urban economy. According to Rajbir, a Jat man in his late-forties:

> When my sons come home and speak in English, it makes me happy that unlike me they will be able to do business with city folks (*shahri babus*). Our parents did not think about educating us; so we are only informally educated. They did not anticipate the DDA takeover of our land and believed that we will be farmers forever. But now as you can see, things have changed. We need educated men to run our businesses and to survive in this city. Every day, I have to deal with customers who speak English or sometimes a government officer comes to my shop and gives me a notice written in English. I need some help in dealing with this new world where people don't speak my language. I am too old to learn English, but it is not too late for my sons. That is why I am educating them in one of the most expensive English-mediums schools in the area.

Unlike the uniformity of opinion regarding the need to educate boys, considerable disagreement exists regarding the extent to which girls should be educated. In addition to the concern about educating daughters in English-medium schools and exposing them to a "corrupt and dangerous" urban environment, Jat parents fear that a daughter's emerging sexuality, immodest behavior, and possible sexual indiscretion could bring dishonor to the family. Many parents said that it was difficult to find a suitable match in rural Haryana for an educated Jat girl and did not see any benefit in educating their daughters beyond the village school. In their view, the learning experience of a daughter should be limited to a level that prepares her to assist in her children's education and to write letters to relatives and friends. The learning experience should not exceed the level beyond which the girl forms her own opinions and begins to express her choices. They believe that a girl with too much education will be combative (*jhagralu*) and less likely to obey the directives of her husband and parents-in-law.

These views on education for girls are compatible with those of the rural agricultural Jat community in Haryana where Shahargaon girls will be sent as brides. Haryana Jats want brides who are amenable to their peasant lifestyle. According to Prem Chowdhry (1994):

> Education is considered to be something that can destroy the concept of agricultural work as a moral duty, as well as women's so-called inborn affinity for agricultural work. The rural regions see the young and educated males who are increasingly reluctant to perform any menial work. Educated females are considered to have the same attitude. This is one of the reasons why education for women is universally decried in rural areas (Chowdhry 1994: 207).

Older Jat women in Shahargaon are the most vocal critics of younger women who want to be educated or want their daughters to be educated. Contrary to the majority view in the village, several Jat parents told me that educated daughters are likely to marry educated men who will allow them a degree of economic independence and personal autonomy. Hemlata, a Jat woman in her forties, wants to make sure that her daughter Usha continues her education beyond the secondary level. In 1999, at the time of the interview, Usha was 15 years old, doing well in school and expressing a strong desire to continue her studies. She pleaded with her parents for their permission to enroll in a university. Against the wishes of the elders in the family, especially her mother-in-law, Hemlata sent Usha to a local college affiliated with the University of Delhi. Hemlata stated her opinion that Jat girls should receive a good education:

> If the village boys can go to school, so can the girls. I think education is very important. And I don't think an educated girl cannot live happily in a farming family. I am educated up to the primary level, but I wish I was more educated. I had a hard time helping my children do their homework. My daughter will be able to educate her children and she will make a good mother. An educated person is a sophisticated person and can plan for her future and that of her children.

Although a minority voice in 1999, Hemlata is one among an increasing number of Jats in Shahargaon calling for a change in attitude toward educating girls. Over the last thirteen years, I have observed this change slowly taking place. In the rapidly transformed socioeconomic context of Shahargaon, Jat parents are beginning to understand that a well-educated mother will improve the chances of survival and well-being of her children. However, their continuing desire to satisfy Haryana Jat families who prefer traditionally modest brides presents a continuing barrier to educating girls in Shahargaon.

TRADITIONAL MARRIAGE AND PRESTIGE

Shahargaon's strategic location and the improved economic status of Jat families have enhanced their opportunity to find marriage partners among affluent Jat families both in Haryana and in New Delhi. Nevertheless, Shahargaon Jats continue to prefer the same Jat villages in Haryana for arranging marriages for their sons and daughters (see Figure 2.8 on page 33).

Haryana Jats now consider marrying into Shahargaon Jats as a hypergamous alliance. In contrast to discrimination and rejection of Shahargaon Jats by Haryana Jats during the early settlement period, landholding Jat families in Haryana are now aggressively seeking marital alliances with Shahargaon Jat families. Improved economic status and Shahargaon's location in the capital city have made Shahargaon Jats desirable partners for establishing marital and business alliances. Shahargaon Jat families often can provide substantial dowry for a daughter's marriage to a suitable groom from a wealthy landholding Haryana family. In recent years, the demand for dowry by Haryana Jats has increased. Because of their improved economic status, Shahargaon Jats have been able to fulfill escalating dowry demands and to ensure a desirable hypergamous alliance for their daughters. In addition to large sums of money, dowry demands include furniture and other household goods, electronic gadgets, clothes, utensils and kitchen appliances, and gold jewelry. Sohan Lal explained:

> The total amount of money spent on dowry can be as high as half of a family's total annual income. Unlike in the past, our families can fulfill these demands without having to borrow money from moneylenders. Given our prestige in the Haryana Jat community we have give to fulfill these demands. If we give a large dowry, our daughter will be happy in her husband's home. Otherwise, she will be harassed and insulted by her mother-in-law and sisters-in-law that she did not bring a good dowry or that she comes from a poor family. We cannot stand this kind of insult.

Marrying daughters into Haryana Jat families has proven to be successful and profitable for Shahargaon Jats in gaining social prestige, in maintaining a traditional Jat identity, and in expanding social network in the region. These alliances allow the Jat community to remain connected with their historical community roots.

In return, Haryana families are willing to pay large dowries for marrying their daughters in Shahargaon Jat families. The financial resources of Shahargaon Jat families and facility of their sons in adapting to an urban business environment makes them desirable marriage partners for girls from Haryana. By bringing traditional Jat brides from rural Haryana into their urbanizing village, Shahargaon Jat parents are ensuring the continuity of their historical traditions associated with their peasant past. However, they also demand substantial dowries from Haryana Jats. In some cases, these demands might include a car for the groom or cash investment in a family business.

Shahargaon's urban surroundings, although economically and socially advantageous, represent a threat to the traditional Jat identity and sense of unity. Shahargaon Jats respond to this threat by choosing wives from rural Haryana to reinforce traditions associated with their former agricultural way of life. By imposing restrictions on women's mobility and economic activities, Shahargaon Jats gain social status and respect from rural Jat families in Haryana. By reinforcing women's seclusion, Shahargaon Jats maintain their traditional rural peasant identity and prevent their unity as an ethnic group from fragmenting in a modern capitalist urban context. By educating their sons and encouraging them to adapt to the urban environment, Shahargaon Jat parents are gaining financial security not only for their old age, but also for their children. By conservatively raising their daughters and limiting their education, they are ensuring the continuity of Jat culture in Shahargaon.

Urbanization has led to an overall improvement in the economic status of Jat families in Shahargaon. However, some members of the community, especially the poor Jats, feel the changes associated with urbanization have come at a cost. They feel that by abandoning an agricultural way of life and by adapting to the urban ways, the Shahargaon Jats have embarked upon and uncertain future. They are the most conservative in protecting their ethnic identity and avoiding urban assimilation by reinforcing their identity as peasants. They blame the increasing income gap among Jat families as the leading cause of lack of unity in the community. In contrast, wealthy Jats have adapted more successfully to the urban environment. By virtue of their economic success in the urban market and improved economic status, they can afford to send daughters as brides to, and receive daughters-in-law as brides from, the wealthy Haryana Jat families. In this manner, preferred marriage patterns promote a traditional Jat unity between the Shahargaon Jats and their Haryana Jat counterparts. Although rich and poor segments of the Jat community have adapted differently to the urban environment, both seek to maintain the traditions and practices of their ancestors. Underlying their apparent urban sophistication, they remain an isolated and insular village.

Chapter 4

✳

Population Growth and "Missing" Girls

atvir and Dalbir are two tall and heavyset middle-aged Jat men. Satvir teaches
at the local primary school in Shahargaon. Dalbir runs a small stationery shop
in the village market. Both were born in Shahargaon and, like most other Jat men
in the village, they look upon life in urbanizing Shahargaon with considerable
apprehension. "My family goes way back in this village. I don't know how many
generations back, but I know I am a descendent of one of the founding families of
Shahargaon," Dalbir explained, proudly reminiscing about the historical depth of
his roots in Shahargaon. He continued:

> I remember when Shahargaon was a small village. I was young then. I
> guess I am still young, but at that time I was a child. We all lived together
> and Shahargaon families had much closer relationship with each other
> than they do now. Living in this village felt like living in an extended
> family. We related in the same way with our neighbors and relatives.
> There was no difference. We had acres of land, which we used to plough
> and grow lentils, vegetables, and sometimes even wheat. There was
> enough food for everyone because we were so few and we work
> cooperatively.

The above reflections show a sense of nostalgia about the past and capture an
idyllic image, perhaps deceptively so, of village life. This image presents a contrast
to what has happened since the confiscation of village land in the early 1970s.
Satvir's comments focused on deteriorating quality of life in the present-day
Shahargaon:

> Nowadays even I don't know how many people live in Shahargaon. The
> village lanes were never crowded like this. We rarely used to think about

taking the alternate routes while crisscrossing the village lanes, but now we do. There are so many cars parked in the narrow village lanes. Can you believe this, cars in Shahargaon?

Satvir asked a rhetorical question, not particularly anticipating an answer. He looked at Dalbir and both laughed imagining how awkward it would have looked if Shahargaon families had driven cars during the farming days. Both joked about driving to their fields and using a Maruti Suzuki, a popular car in India, to plough the fields. Satvir continued:

> We need to limit the number of people in this village just like we need to do something about the number of people living in this city or for that matter in this country. Our village is just like India, bursting at its boundaries with people everywhere. Our life here is a showcase of what is happening in India. We are such a small village, I mean in terms of size, but we have too many people, too many cars, too much trash, too many problems, and no solutions. We need to have small families. I think each family should have only one or two children at the most. If we keep growing in number like this, very soon we will run out of space to live. There will not be any land left for us to live on.

Shahargaon has indeed become a crowded place with too many people and vehicles occupying narrow village lanes. The population of native Shahargaon residents in the village increased by 24 percent between 1993 and 2003 (Table 4.1), and at the same time the number of non-Shahargaon residents who live in the village as tenants also increased. Since migrant families only live in Shahargaon for a short period and their residence is determined by the available job opportunities in

T A B L E 4.1   Population Growth in Shahargaon
(native Shahargaon residents only)

Caste	1993 Households	Population	1999 Households	Population	2003 Households	Population
Brahman (Priest)	3	17	4	21	5	27
Jat (Agriculturalist)	131	782	157	889	179	938
Kumhar (Potter)	5	20	5	27	5	28
Nai (Barber)	10	70	13	85	15	92
Chamar (Leatherworker)	10	68	12	83	13	91
Harijan (Sweeper)	19	117	23	140	28	160
Total	178	1074	214	1245	245	1336

the area, I found it difficult to estimate the precise number of tenant families living in the village. Most of the these families are "outsiders" and unskilled immigrants from the neighboring states of Uttar Pradesh, Bihar, and West Bengal, looking for low-wage employment in New Delhi. Shahargaon Jats regard these tenants as temporary residents having little interest in becoming a part of the village community. In order to take advantage of the demand for rental space, many Jat families have converted ground-level rooms in their homes into small rental units. Meanwhile, they have moved into smaller space on the second floor and/or built additional residential space for themselves on top of their existing homes. Upon entering the narrow lanes of the village, I could see a tall maze of crudely constructed new additions on top of old houses. Huge billboards in close proximity, with a variety of colors, shapes, and luminosity hang on the outside walls of the houses. Some closely-spaced billboards gave the impression that they were screaming at each other in the competition to call attention to their products. Space has become a luxury. Amidst the intrusion of the outside world, villagers live in increasingly crowded quarters at the edge of the mega city that surrounds them.

INDIA'S POPULATION: MORE THAN ONE BILLION PEOPLE

The transformed village of Shahargaon is a microcosm of the larger National Capital Territory of New Delhi—a region of roughly 13.7 million people with a population density of 24,071 per square mile. Shahargaon also provides a snapshot of India—a country of more than one billion people experiencing rapid social change brought about by what is commonly referred to as "globalization." Between 1965 and 2004, India's population has doubled from 500 million to slightly more than one billion. By the year 2030, India will surpass China to become the most populous country in the world (Table 4.2). Both India and China have at least three times more people than does the United States, the third most populous country in the world.

In his classic monograph entitled *India's Population: Fact and Policy*, S. Chandrasekhar (1946), an Indian demographer who later became the Union Minister of Health and Family Planning, warned that India's population may reach the "staggering figure of 700 million by 2001" (Chandrasekhar 1946: 15).

T A B L E 4.2   Top Ten Most Populous Countries in the World

Country	Population (in millions)
China	1,313.6
India	1,095.3
USA	298.4
Indonesia	245.4
Brazil	188.1
Pakistan	165.8
Bangladesh	147.3
Russia	142.8
Nigeria	131.8
Japan	127.4

SOURCE: US Census Bureau, International Database, 2005)

Interestingly, the 2001 Indian census figures indicate that Chandrasekhar's prediction of a "staggering" Indian population was an underestimation. India's population reached one billion in 2001—1,027,015,247 to be precise (Census of India 2001). Approximately 16 percent of the world's population lives in India. Between 1991 and 2001, its population increased by 21.34 percent, and on average it grows by 155 million people per year, 12.7 million per month, 42,434 per day, 1,768 per hour, and twenty-nine per minute (Census of India 2001).

NATIONAL POPULATION POLICY

In this section I provide a brief overview of Indian government policies aimed at slowing population growth. My purpose is to provide a policy context for the Indian government's involvement in designing and implementing population control policies, media campaigns, and population control slogans advocating the benefits of a small family. In the late 1970s, the popular slogan "a small family is a happy family" (*chota parivar sukhi parivar*), became a familiar endorsement for birth control. The slogan usually appeared along with the accompanying image of a red triangle containing the happy faces of a couple with two children. Today it continues to decorate village walls. This slogan and many other media campaigns advocating a "small and happy family" have strongly influenced the concept of ideal family size in India, and in Shahargaon.

After independence from British rule in 1947, Indian policy makers became concerned about unchecked growth of the country's population. They recognized that the country's population could be either its biggest liability or its greatest asset. In 1952, just five years after independence, the country established the world's first national Family Planning Program, more recently known as the Family Welfare Program. This program called for a nationwide effort to increase the standard of living by controlling population growth. As part of the program, the government sponsored several initiatives with the objective of reducing birth rate to a level consistent with the national economic needs and development goals. In the mid-1970s, the government adopted a National Population Policy that proposed, among other goals, an integrated approach toward reducing the birth rate by promoting the use of contraceptives. During the late 1970s, it even went to the extreme of launching a highly unpopular campaign of forced sterilization (Gwatkin 1979). People all over the country revolted against Prime Minister Indira Gandhi's government for using the state machinery to implement this campaign.

During the next two decades, the government engaged in less coercive but goal-directed policies and methods for reducing the rate of population growth. In the late 1990s it revised the National Population Policy to include the goal of promoting reproductive health. The revised policy, adopted in 2000, has now become a cornerstone of government efforts to control population growth. Its major provisions include improving health care infrastructure, making contraceptive methods easily available, and promoting integrated service delivery for reproductive and child health care (Census of India 2000). The government has made available all contraceptive methods and family planning services free of charge.

Although the crude birth rate (number of births per thousand people) has declined from forty in 1970 to twenty-four in 2001 (Census of India 2000), the present government still views India's fertility level as too high with a slower-than-expected rate of decline. The revised National Population Policy has provided for massive media and public information campaigns to control population growth, an effective employment strategy to create jobs and provide economic growth, and incentives to married couples to adopt two-child or small family norm. The policy represents a comprehensive approach to simultaneously address interrelated issues of reproductive health, child survival, and family planning. The centerpiece of this policy is to educate communities and promote their active involvement in family planning programs.

FAMILY PLANNING IN SHAHARGAON

Since the 1990s, Shahargaon residents have had access to contraceptives and family counseling services at the state-funded Primary Health Center (PHC) located in the town of Mandi (Figure 4.1). In addition to providing free contraceptives to clients, the Primary Health Center offers a variety of prenatal and postnatal care services. Two men from the Harijan community in Shahargaon are employed at the local government hospital located just five miles to the northeast of the village. Shahargaon families often use these men as "inside contacts" to access health care services at the local hospital. As part of the state sponsored Maternal and Child Health (MCH) program and the Integrated Child Development Scheme (ICDS),

FIGURE 4.1   Map showing the location of Shahargaon and Mandi
(© Sunil K. Khanna)

Shahargaon has a health worker (*anganwadi*) and an Auxiliary Nurse Midwife (ANM) to advise and provide basic health care to pregnant women. The health worker lives in the village, maintains child immunization records, prenatal care reports, and provides free contraceptives, and family planning advice.

In 2003, I conducted in-depth interviews with a random sample of 58 married Jat couples in the village. I collected information on age at marriage and first pregnancy, and preferences regarding family size and sex composition. Married men and women showed a high level of awareness and acceptance of temporary methods (condoms, Copper-T, and oral pills) and permanent methods (vasectomy and tubectomy) of contraception. Although the views of my informants did not vary by socioeconomic status, they did vary by age. To better explain this variability, I have categorized married Jat couples who participated in the survey into the following two age groups:

> *Group I (60 years or older)*: I interviewed 25 couples in this age category. A majority of women in this group had completed their reproductive span by the mid- to late 1970s before the availability of family planning methods in the village.

> *Group II (Younger than 60 years)*: I interviewed 33 couples in this age category. Women in this group were either recently married or had not completed their reproductive span by the mid- to late 1970s. When they were young they were targets for state-sponsored family planning campaigns and had easy access to family planning methods.

Most noticeably, couples in Group I married at an earlier age and had lower levels of acceptance of family planning methods than those in Group II. In keeping with the tradition of early marriage for girls among Haryana Jats, families in Shahargaon arrange marriages before girls reach 18 years of age. Marriages among Jats mark the formalization of alliances between two individuals and their families, but the bride and groom do not consummate their relationship until after being married for two or three years. As described in Chapter 2, the ceremony of consummation (*gauna*) signals the beginning of sexual relations between married couples. Among peasant communities in north India, this ceremony marks the time when the bride begins living in her husband's home (Minturn 1993; Wadley 1994).

Jats in Shahargaon prefer that married couples consummate their relationship before they are 20 years old, not longer than two years after marriage. Parents rationalize their preference for early marriage and consummation as a way of minimizing the "corrupting" influence of the urban world on their daughters. The average age of consummation among women in Group I was 16 years of age. Women in this group rarely mentioned using temporary methods of contraception. In their experience, family planning was synonymous with sterilization performed after they had achieved desired family size. They believed that the burden of limiting family size was to be entirely born by women and that men were incapable of being responsible for family planning. Women were more likely than their husbands to choose sterilization to limit family size. Group I couples rarely used temporary methods of contraception for child spacing. According to Sharbati, a Jat woman in her sixties:

> When I had my fourth child I decided that I did not want to have any more children. My mother-in-law did not like my decision. She told my husband and then he was mad at me. He told me that he wanted at least one more child. He said it was his mother's wish to have a house full of kids. I knew I could not manage more children. Four children are a lot. But I did not have the courage to argue with my husband or ask him permission to go for a sterilization operation [*nasbandi*]. I contacted Pyari [the village midwife] for help. She took me to a lady doctor at the hospital. The lady doctor was very nice to me and told me that I could bring my husband along to the sterilization operation. I told her that my husband did not want it, but I was ready for it. She asked me to come a week later for the operation. I went back home and talked with my husband. I am a strong-headed woman. I argued with my husband but I did it in a respectful manner. He finally accepted my decision and gave me permission to undergo the procedure.

Sharbati's comments show that Jat women could be forceful with their husbands in arguing for sterilization once they believed they have achieved a desired family size. According to Pyari (Figure 4.2), the village midwife:

> Until the 1980s, more women than men cared about limiting family size. Jat families used to be large with three or four children per family. Some families in the village even had five or six children. Since in those days many families lived in the same house, it was difficult to tell how many children each married couple had in the household. Jat men showed little interest in using family planning methods for avoiding pregnancy or even for increasing the gap between two children. I know from other women in the village that their husbands never agreed to using condoms. Jat men rarely agreed to a sterilization operation [*nasbandi*] for their wives. But things began to change after the 1980s. Job insecurity led many to think about limiting family size or living separately from their parents or relatives. Nowadays younger Jat men are open to using condoms, but they do not want to be sterilized [*nasbandi*]. They also strongly oppose to the idea of their wives seeking sterilization.

In comparison to Group I couples, the average age at consummation for women in Group II was 17.5 years. The younger Jat couples of Group II expressed a strong preference for using temporary methods of contraception for spacing their children, and still did not favor sterilization. Among the younger couples in this group, more women were more likely than men to use contraceptives. Younger

FIGURE 4.2   Pyari, a midwife in Shahargaon (© Sunil K. Khanna)

women reported that they received information on the available methods of family planning from the village midwife or village health worker. They complained that village health workers only targeted women for promoting the use of family planning methods and that men rarely received any such admonitions from government officials. Family planning records I examined at the Mandi Primary Health Center confirm that family planning workers have mostly targeted women for promoting the use of both temporary and permanent methods of contraception. According to Bano, a 32-year-old Jat woman:

> My husband is not concerned about family planning. He thinks I know all that needs to be done and he trusts me. When I was pregnant with my first child, the village health worker told me about family planning methods. When I visited the Mandi PHC [Primary Health Center], the nurse [Auxiliary Nurse Midwife or ANM] also told me about family planning. I told her that she should also talk with my husband. She said they don't have men working on promoting family planning at the PHC. So, it

would be difficult for a woman to talk to a man about using family planning methods. I believe that men too should be informed about family planning methods. They should be responsible for limiting family size.

Bano's comments illustrate women's general unhappiness that family planning programs have focused primarily on women.

PREFERRED FAMILY SIZE

Older Jat couples of Group I who had little exposure to family planning campaigns stated that they prefer to have at least four children per family, ideally two boys and two girls. When they were young, family planning services were available only at the Mandi Public Health Clinic, and they did not have an easy access to modern methods of contraception. Up to the 1970s the Shahargaon Jat community was engaged primarily in agriculture which made large families advantageous. In contrast, a large majority of Group II younger couples preferred two or three children per family, ideally a boy and a girl or two boys and a girl. A few couples preferred only two children per family, ideally two boys or a boy and a girl. More Jat women than men preferred a gender-balanced family composition, i.e. to have at least one girl in the family. Mange Ram, a 37-year-old Jat man, worked as an electrician with a local electricity company. He believed that the Indian government was right in recommending that people should limit family size to only two children per family. When I asked him about preferred family size in Shahargaon, he responded in an assertive tone:

> Look around here, how many children do you see? There are children everywhere. How are we going to clothe and feed them? How will we find schools to educate them? How will all of them find work? A family with more than two children is more likely to be poor than a family with two or fewer children. I cannot think of any reason why one should have a large family these days. We just cannot afford a large family any more. I have two sons and my wife and I do not want any more children. Our goal is to educate them so that they can find a better future for themselves. I do not want them to work as daily wage laborers like so many do in this village. I want them to find well-paying permanent private or government jobs.

Mange Ram's views reflect a majority opinion in the village. He echoes a pragmatic view of the advantages of a small family in a village where agriculture is no longer the primary means of livelihood. However, older Jat men believe that the government has no right to interfere in parents' decision regarding family size. Chandarbhan, a Jat man in his mid-sixties, runs a furniture shop in Shahargaon's urban market. He stated:

> I do not trust the government, especially not after the program to forcibly sterilize people in the 1970s. The government has never done anything

good for us. Government officers are corrupt. I have heard that village health workers get cash incentives for cases of sterilization they bring to the government hospitals. Why should I help them? We should have at least four children per family; three of them should be boys. We need boys to deal with New Delhi and to run our businesses. God has given us enough money to feed our children and to educate them. People should not stop having children simply because they are poor. I know having more children means having more mouths to feed. But it also means having more working hands.

Although Chandarbhan voices a minority opinion, difference in family size preferences often became topics for contentious debates between older and younger Jat men. While older men believe that large family size will ensure the continuity of the Jat community, younger men regard a large family as a financial burden further complicating their lives.

Shahargaon Jats make decisions regarding family size informed by their everyday circumstances and the influence of their peasant history and culture. They often struggle to reconcile the ideals of their peasant Jat lifestyle with the realities of their everyday existence in urban New Delhi. Sohan Lal eloquently captured these contradictions:

When we were agriculturalists, we needed hands to work in the fields. We needed more men to protect our land and our families. A family with more men was not only considered rich but also politically powerful. As they say among the Jats of Haryana—the number of sons is equal to the number of sticks and the number of sticks determines the amount of land a family can control. We all lived by these words. So in those days people preferred to have large families. But now that we are no longer agriculturalists we need to adapt to this new world. We can no longer afford to have large families. We need small families, but we have to remember that we are peasants.

Following Shahargaon's urban assimilation and the confiscation of its agricultural land, the desire to limit family size has become strong. The average number of members per household has decreased from 6 in 1993 to 5.2 in 2003. Married couples now have a high level of awareness of and easy access to the means to limit family size. Women are especially well informed about the various contraceptive methods and can obtain them privately and free of cost from the nearby Primary Health Center in Mandi.

The high acceptance of contraceptives is due to several factors—the shift from a rural subsistence system to a commercial economy, exposure to state-promoted media campaigns advocating small families, and easy availability of family planning methods. Married couples have adopted the government slogan "a small family is a happy family" (*chota parivar sukhi parivar*) as a key to their prosperity and symbolic of their new "urban" (*shahri*) identity (Figure 4.3). A majority of Jat men and women talk about the disadvantages of a large family in terms of the need for more

FIGURE 4.3   A billboard displaying benefits of a small family

(SOURCE: Voluntary Health Association of India.)

resources to feed, clothe, and educate their children, and for more space within their houses. Married couples often increased their use of contraceptives after they had achieved a family of desired size and sex composition. I heard of only a few cases of unintentional pregnancies that resulted from not using contraceptives.

"MISSING" WOMEN

A remarkable characteristic of India's population is a masculine sex ratio, which means that the country's population has more men than women. India shares this characteristic with other agrarian countries in the South East Asian Region (SEAR). Two common elements characterize these countries—a rigid sexual division of labor, and highly differentiated gender roles. Census records show that India's sex ratio has been consistently masculine since 1881 when India began counting its people. According to the most recent census figures in 2001, India's sex ratio is 933, which the Indian government describes as a "welcome improvement" in comparison to 927, the sex ratio recorded in 1991 (Census of India 2001). Nevertheless, India's sex ratio has remained masculine for all census years since 1901 (Table 4.3).

Interest in sex ratios goes back to the days of British colonial occupation. As early as the late 1800s, the British government, expressed concerned that female infanticide might be responsible for the masculine child sex ratio recorded in some communities (Bhatnagar et al. 2005; Pakrasi 1970; Pakrasi and Haldar 1971). In 1882, under the direction of the Inspector-General of Registration in Bengal, the

T A B L E 4.3   India's Total Population and Sex Ratios (1901–2001)

Census Year	Total Population (in millions)	Sex Ratio (females per 1000 males)
1901	238	972
1911	252	964
1921	251	955
1931	278	950
1941	318	945
1951	361	946
1961	439	941
1971	548	930
1981	683	934
1991	846	927
2001	1028 (or 1.02 billion)	933

SOURCE: Census of India, 2001)

British government collected and collated census records on living conditions and sex ratios (Census of India 2001).

National census data on the sex ratios shows that northern and western states have more masculine sex ratios than southern and eastern states (Figure 4.4). The

F I G U R E 4.4   Jat parents playing with their son (© Sunil K. Khanna)

north Indian state of Haryana, the parent state of the Shahargaon Jats, has the lowest (most masculine) sex ratio of 861 females per 1000 males (Census of India 2001). Nobel laureate Amartya Sen (1990, 2003) caused quite a stir by suggesting that excess female mortality in Asian countries, especially India and China, has led to 100 million fewer women (or "missing" women) in the world's total population. In a more recent article published in 2003 in the *British Medical Journal*, Sen shows that a slight reduction in female mortality between 1990 and 2003 was counterbalanced by an increase in female selective abortion. Sen's phrase "missing women" recently has become not only a powerful descriptor for the marginalized status of Indian women, but also a slogan motivating efforts to raise their status.

The sex ratio of India's child population in age group 0-6 is 927, which means 927 girls per 1,000 boys, in comparison to the child sex ratio of 945 recorded in 1991. This comparison indicates a significant decline in the number of girls in comparison to boys in this age category. Assuming that the natural sex ratio at birth (number females/number of males x 1000) ranges between 971 and 952, the 2001 census data on sex ratios shows a significant deficit of females. A recently published report—"State of World's Children"—by the UNICEF states that the masculine trend observed in India's sex ratio has been consistently increasing since the 1950s (Table 4.4). The report further suggests that sex ratios in almost 80 percent of India's 593 districts suggests significantly more boys than girls in the under age five age group (UNICEF 2007).

While Sen (1990) has used the label "missing women," Coale (1991) has used the slogan "missing females" and explains the reason for the deficit as follows:

> ...extensive reading of demographic and ethnographic studies...suggest that Sen's "missing women" and Coale's "missing females" could more aptly be referred to as "missing girls", given that it is excessive female mortality before birth, at birth, and in infancy and childhood which more than any other factor accounts for the imbalance in sex ratios...(Croll 2000: 2).

Researchers have suggested that a large majority of parents consider sons as economic and social assets and daughters as liabilities (Arokiasamy 2007; Jeffery and Jeffery 1996). In comparison to daughters, sons receive better education, health care, and opportunities for growth in life. Several studies have measured the effect of this bias in causing high mortality and morbidity rates among girls (Basu 1992; Das Gupta 1987; Wadley 1994), indicating that more girls than boys are dying in India.

T A B L E 4.4   Total Sex Ratios and Child Sex Ratios in India (1951–2001)

Year	Total Sex Ratio	Child Sex Ratio
1951	946	983
1961	941	976
1971	930	964
1981	934	962
1991	927	945
2001	933	927

SOURCE: Census of India 2001)

"MISSING GIRLS" IN SHAHARGAON

In this section I present evidence of "missing girls" in Shahargaon and examine cultural explanations for increasing demographic imbalance. I collected my own local census data in 1993, 1999, and 2003, the results showing a steady decline in the number of females relative to the number of males (Table 4.5). While the total Jat population in the village has steadily increased from 782 in 1993 to 938 in 2003 (an increase of roughly 17 percent), sex ratios of females to males during the same period show a declining trend—from 840 in 1993 to 797 in 2003 (Figure 4.5). Sex ratios in the child population (0-6 years) show a precipitous decline in the number of girls from 710 per 1000 boys in 1993 to 597 per 1000 boys in 2003 (Table 4.6).

FIGURE 4.5   A Jat mother holding her newborn son (© Sunil K. Khanna)

T A B L E 4.5   Sex Ratios among Shahargaon Jats (1993–2003)

Year	Total Population	Males	Females	Sex Ratio
1993	782	425	357	840
1999	889	490	399	814
2003	938	522	416	797

T A B L E 4.6   Sex Ratios in 0–1 years and 0–6 years age groups (1993–2003)

	0–1 Years				0–6 Years			
Year	Total Population	Boys	Girls	Sex Ratio	Total Population	Boys	Girls	Sex Ratio
1993	26	16	10	625	183	107	76	710
1999	25	17	8	470	193	137	56	409
2003	19	12	7	583	107	67	40	597

T A B L E 4.7   Sex Ratio in Child Population (0–6 years) in Select States/ Regions in India

State/Region	1991	2001
India	945	927
Haryana	879	819
Delhi	915	868
Shahargaon	710 (1993)	597 (2003)

SOURCE: Census of India 2001)

T A B L E 4.8   Sex Ratio in Child Population (0–6 years) in Three Economic Groups in Shahargaon (2003)

Group	Females	Males	Sex Ratio
A	32	21	656
B	16	9	563
C	19	10	526

T A B L E 4.9   Revised Sex Ratios (including reported cases of death) for 0–6 years age group (1993–2003)

	0–6 Years		
Year	Boys	Girls	Sex Ratio
1993	113	85	752
1999	145	69	476
2003	72	51	708

The 0–1 age category shows an excess of boys over girls in all the three census years. The lowest recorded sex ratio (470 girls per 1000 boys) in this age category was in the year 1999.

The sex ratio in the Shahargaon Jat child population is skewed toward male even more than shown in regional and national trends (Table 4.7).

In 2003, the sex ratios in the child population (0–6 years) showed a clear trend across three economic groups identified earlier (Table 4.8). The sex ratio was alarmingly masculine in the three groups, however, it was worst in Group C (low income) households in comparison to Group A (affluent households) and Group B (middle income households).

The number of girls relative to the number of boys is higher among relatively wealthy families who can better afford the "luxury" of raising girls. As described in Chapter 3, women in Group A and B households are slightly better educated and more informed about health care than those in Group C households. Although there may be an unequal distribution of households resources favoring boys and discriminating against girls, these characteristics were rarely reported as leading to the death of girls. Jat parents, regardless of their economic status, are able to fulfill the basic demands of food and health care for their children. Finally, the reported cases of deaths of children in the 0–6 years category are too small to have a significant impact on sex ratio in the child population. Given the above explanation, we must consider the likelihood that prenatal sex selection contributes to the skewing of child sex ratio leading to "missing" girls in Shahargaon's population.

In order to examine the effect of child morality on sex ratios in the 0–6 year age group, I recalculated by adding the reported number of deaths of boys and girls (Table 4.9). Since girls died more often than boys, the ratio of girls to boys born in the village is higher in each year.

However, these figures are still skewed in favor of males. By extrapolating from the average sex ratio in the world, which is 990 females to 1000 males (Sen 1990), I estimate that Shahargaon has twenty girls "missing" from birth in its child population (0–6 years). If we extrapolate from India's sex ratio of 933 females to 1000 males in 2001, Shahargaon still has 16 "missing" girls in the 0–6 years age group. In the absence of any other reported explanation by Jat parents, son preference and sex-selective abortion of female fetuses is the most plausible explanation for this discrepancy.

OPINIONS ABOUT "MISSING" GIRLS

In Shahargaon, at every stage in the lifecycle—from birth to old age—Jat men hold a higher social position and have more decision making power than Jat women. This culturally ascribed status allows them to manipulate the system to their advantage. Men's opinions tend to provide the framework for decisions about age at marriage, timing of pregnancy, child spacing, use of contraceptive methods, family size, and sex composition. Jat families celebrate the birth of a son and announce it with pride to the entire village. In contrast, they quietly inform close relatives and neighbors about the birth of a daughter. Premwati, a Jat woman in her seventies, showed me her grandson with pride. "This is my lottery," she said in an excited voice. She added:

> I am so happy that now both my sons have sons of their own. Our family name and honor in this village are now immortal. I can now die in peace. God has given me everything. I have three grandsons and I don't need anything else. My eldest son already has two sons of his own, but I was worried about my younger son. This is his first son. God has heard my prayers and has blessed me with a grandson. I am a very lucky grandmother.

Premwati's extended family shares her feelings about her sons and grandsons. In Shahargaon, a Jat family gains honor and respect by having sons. The number of sons is symbolic of the social and political strength of the family. A family without sons is considered unfortunate and weak. In expressing her elation Premwati noticeably did not mention that she has two granddaughters. Unlike sons, villagers regard daughters as temporary residents in the homes of their parents. After marriage they leave their parents' homes and live with their husbands' families. Parents believe that the expense of raising a daughter is a gift that will belong to her husband. A woman's natal family also has to bear the cost of her wedding and, more importantly, her dowry. Daughters are neither expected to take care of their aging parents nor perform any religious rights in their natal homes. Jat parents say their unmarried daughters are, "commodities or assets that belong to someone else" (*paraya dhan*).

Son preference in Shahargaon has intensified, as shown above by increasingly skewed sex ratios, along with its assimilation into the urban metropolis of New Delhi. The desire for smaller families creates more pressure to give birth to boys to create all-sons or one-son-one-daughter families. Sulekha was 24 years old in the second month of pregnancy with her second child. Since she already had a 3-year-old daughter, she wanted her next child to be a boy. She explained her views:

> I am happy that I have a daughter; I love my daughter. But I want my next child to be a son. I only want to have two children. We simply can't afford three children. I don't have a choice. I have to make sure that this child is a son. My husband agrees with me and so does my mother-in-law. Only a son would complete our family. I will do whatever it takes to give birth to a son.

Sons are important to maintain Premwati's family honor and to complete Sulekha's family. Such expressions of strong son preference prevail in a number of similar stories I collected from Jat men and women in Shahargaon. These stories also underscore another important theme, i.e. Shahargaon Jats no longer strive for a large family in order to maximize the possibility for having sons. The availability of birth control technologies, family planning campaigns, and the intrusion of the city into the village have created circumstances favorable for maintaining smaller families and for raising sons, but are still unfavorable for raising daughters. The recent decline in the number of girls born in the village marks the emergence of a new trend not previously recognized by demographers—a trend in which a decrease in the rate of population growth and a decline in the number of girls relative to the number of boys are occurring simultaneously.

Chapter 5

✳

Global Technologies and Local Implications

"New reproductive technologies," especially ultrasonography and amniocentesis, provide dynamic images of the prenatal world that help physicians in diagnosing conception, identifying fetal abnormalities, and monitoring fetal growth. These technologies were first developed and refined during the 1960s in Europe and the United States. By the early 1970s, obstetricians and gynecologists in non-western countries were routinely using them. Government hospitals and private clinics in India started offering ultrasonography and amniocentesis in the mid-1970s. By the late 1980s, private clinics launched massive advertising campaigns specifically promoting ultrasonography as a "miracle" technology for prenatal identification of fetal sex. Advertisements in newspapers and roadside billboards offering married couples a reliable means to find out the sex of the fetus were visible all over the country, and especially in urban areas. This publicity in a society that has traditionally preferred sons over daughters effectively fixed in people's minds that ultrasonography was a means for prenatal sex identification and had no other prescriptive medical purposes. Parents desiring sons over daughters started using ultrasonography in combination with female-selective abortion to avoid the birth of an unwanted daughter. This coupling of ultrasonography with sex-selective abortion shows how local culture redefines a new technology in the context of traditions, individual preferences, and market-driven forces.

Social researchers, medical practitioners, policy makers, and social activists agree that new reproductive technologies should be available for purposes that provide medical benefits to their users. However, they disagree on how to separate the intended medical use of the technologies from their social use for prenatal sex identification and sex-selective abortion. Despite a chorus of competing views on the use of ultrasonography, existing understanding of these issues has been mostly limited to journalistic accounts or scholarly writings based on secondary data. A few investigators have studied the incidence of female feticide primarily from clinical data (Booth et al. 1994; Jeffery et al. 1984; Patel 1989; Ramanamma and

Bambawale 1980). They have used clinical records on the number of female fetuses aborted at a particular medical facility as proxy indicator of female-selective abortion. Although significant in pointing out that more female fetuses than male fetuses are aborted in India, such studies lack evidence to show that parents actually sought female-selective abortions after parental sex identification. Since India does not have an effective abortion data registration system, a large number of abortions occur in clinics that neither keep reliable records of abortions nor report their cases for inclusion in government databases.

Researchers who have examined regional and national demographic data trends suggest that a sharp increase in the number of boys relative to the number of girls at birth and in the child population (0-6 years) indicates an increasing incidence of female-selective abortion (Bhat and Zavier 2007; Fred et al. 2002; Sudha and Rajan 1999). They use masculine sex ratio trends as a proxy measure for strength of son preference as well as for the incidence of female-selective abortion. In the reporting of their work, however, key questions on important issues remain unanswered—why does son preference continue to exist in India? How do people learn about the sex of the fetus? How do they access and use ultrasonography for prenatal sex identification or abortion services for seeking female-selective abortion? Who makes the decision to use ultrasonography, or for that matter, how accessible and affordable is this technology?

In this chapter, I expand upon the above issues by first providing a brief overview of new reproductive technologies, including ultrasonography, currently available in Shahargaon and surrounding areas. First, I discuss the opinions of local doctors, especially obstetricians and radiologists who offer ultrasonography in their practices. Second, I provide a brief overview of the scientific and medical foundations of new reproductive technologies. Understanding the medical and technological background of these technologies provides the context for examining how their purposes derive from social context. Third, I present qualitative data— knowledge, experiences, and opinions pertaining to the availability and use of ultrasonography by married couples in Shahargaon. I will contrast the prevailing medical discourse with users' understandings of the technology exclusively in terms of its benefits in identifying the sex of the fetus. The perspective of users reveals the fallacy of simply labeling ultrasonography as a scientifically objective and gender-neutral reproductive technology.

"MIRACLE" TECHNOLOGY IN PRENATAL
DIAGNOSTIC CLINICS

Shahargaon has thirteen medical centers distributed among three small shopping plazas and an outlying residential colony. These centers include primary care clinics, multispecialty clinics providing obstetrics, gynecology, and birthing services, and diagnostic clinics offering pathology, ultrasonography, and radiology services. Four of the multispecialty clinics also offer diagnostic services including ultrasonography. I contacted doctors, including five specialists in obstetrics and gynecology (OB-GYN), who manage the centers. Four doctors, including one

OB–GYN specialist, refused to speak with me suspecting that I was a journalist or activist whose intention was to write adverse newspaper reports detrimental to their medical practice. They cited fears of harassment by police and activist members of local non–government organizations who suspected that doctors were conducting illegal prenatal sex determination tests. I later learned that these four doctors joined into a tightly knit group and agreed upon a common strategy against social critics. In response to numerous media reports labeling them as "professionals aiding and abetting in crimes against women," they decided not to cooperate with government agencies and activist groups soliciting information about their clinical practice. Other doctors I met were willing to share their opinions on ultrasonography and discussed its medical benefits as well as its use for prenatal sex identification. Two of the nine doctors who responded felt compelled to speak on behalf of the entire medical community suggesting that by virtue of their Hippocratic Oath,[1] they can do no harm to their patients and therefore, will never conduct unethical and illegal prenatal sex determination tests that may result in the killing of girls. However, other doctors were reluctant to deny patients access to ultrasonography, stating that married couples in India have a "right" to choose the sex of their child. Regardless of their differing opinions on sex selection, all doctors with whom I spoke strongly advocated for and used new reproductive technologies, including ultrasonography, in their own practices. They believe that the new technologies hold considerable medical promise. Dr. Arora, an OB–GYN specialist in Shahargaon commented:

> Medical science has finally delivered us a miracle technology. It is called ultrasound [ultrasonography]. It is indeed miraculous to be able to clearly see a developing fetus inside a mother's womb. Before ultrasound physicians had to rely on results of blood tests and other indirect means of assessing the health of the fetus. We used mother's health during pregnancy as a proxy indicator of the health of the fetus because we could not see the intrauterine world. Now that is all history. The new technologies have simply taken guesswork out of our practice. We do not have to rely on guesswork anymore. We can now directly monitor the fetus, progress of pregnancy and labor, and also make therapeutic recommendations on the basis of what we see inside the mother's womb.

Dr. Seth, who runs the New Delhi Diagnostic Clinic in the Shahargaon market, pointed out a difference between a medical practitioner's understanding of ultrasonography and that of a patient seeking ultrasonography services:

> Most people do not understand the potential of ultrasonography. They are not doctors; they did not go to medical school. Most people here are not even well educated. They only see the use from their own vantage point.

---

1. Biomedical practitioners in India, just like biomedical practitioner elsewhere in the world, are bound by the Hippocratic Oath. The Oath expects doctors to always work in the best interest of their patients. It sets specific guidelines for the professional conduct of doctors.

They know that ultrasonography can tell if the woman is pregnant with a boy or a girl. That is the only information they want from ultrasonography. Personally, I think that such a misuse of ultrasonography is tragic, but this is India; many parents here continue to believe that sons are more important than daughters. These are the people who are keeping us from progressing like western nations.

Dr. Seth strongly advocated for the use of ultrasonography because of its medical benefits, especially for monitoring fetal growth, identifying abnormalities in the fetus, and diagnosing complications before childbirth. He identified himself not only as a conscientious doctor, but as a responsible citizen who wants to stop the use of ultrasonography for prenatal sex identification. Dr. Seth explained his views:

In my practice, parents ask me to tell them the sex of the fetus. They ask this question everyday, many times in a day. Even when there was no law against it, I believed that telling the parents about the sex of the fetus was simply wrong. So I never did. Instead, I tried to advise parents not to discriminate against their daughters. Now there is a law against prenatal sex identification. No one knows how the law works, but if doctors use ultrasonography to identify the sex of the fetus, then they can be put in jail and their medical licenses can be suspended. I do not know about other doctors in the area, but I do not engage in such an illegal and unethical act.

In the opinion of health care providers, ultrasonography is a technology that itself has no social purpose or bias, and is a step forward in technological development and innovation in medicine. According to Dr. Seth:

Why ban the new technology? I do not understand the logic behind the Prenatal Diagnostic Techniques Act.[2] Ultrasonography by itself does not kill girls. It does not favor boys or discriminate against girls, but parents do. The job of a doctor is to use ultrasonography to diagnose fetal abnormalities, learn how the pregnancy is progressing, and to monitor the health of the mother and her fetus. Doctors are not evil or greedy. But our government thinks that they are bad and will do anything to

---

2. Several activists/advocacy groups in India strongly oppose the use of ultrasonography for prenatal sex identification claiming that it invariably leads to female-selective abortion. They contend that such a use of ultrasonography represents a "modern" means of realizing the traditional preference for sons and discrimination against daughters in particular and women in general (Patel 1989). In 1994, the Indian government passed the Pre-conceptional and Pre-natal Diagnostic Techniques (Regulation and Prevention of Misuse) Act (hereafter Prenatal Diagnostic Techniques Act or PDTA). The Prenatal Diagnostic Techniques Act came into effect in 1996. It bans the use of ultrasonography and other diagnostic technologies for prenatal sex determination and the practice of sex-selection abortion. In Chapter 7, I provide a detailed discussion of what constitutes the legally-defined "misuse" of ultrasonography associated with the practice of female-selective abortion.

make money. Our government and our people need to be educated about ultrasonography. It makes little sense to ban the technology itself. By banning the use of ultrasonography we are in fact banning medical progress. The government should first get educated about the medical benefits of ultrasonography. Then it should invest its resources in educating parents and getting rid of dowry. This will take away all the reasons for parents to not want girls. The Prenatal Diagnostic Techniques Act has simply created more hurdles in the practice of modern medicine in India. The government or journalists should not demonize the technology itself or for that matter those who offer prenatal diagnostic services.

All nine doctors with whom I spoke overwhelmingly supported unregulated access to ultrasonography. While acknowledging that some profit-driven diagnosticians use ultrasonography for prenatal sex identification, they believe that the medical benefits far outweigh its "misuse". None of the nine doctors admitted to have engaged in a commercial transaction using ultrasonography for sex identification. They placed the blame for "misuse" on parents and strong son preference in Indian society.

PRECISION ULTRASOUND CLINIC

Dr. Geeta Verma is an OB-GYN doctor who runs the Precision Ultrasound Clinic located in a residential neighborhood nearby Shahargaon. Established in 1991 by Dr. Verma, this clinic was the first to offer ultrasound service in the area and has recently started to offer birthing services as well. Most patients of the clinic are either residents of Shahargaon or live in the surrounding area. Amenities of the clinic include a well-equipped medical laboratory, birthing room, X-ray equipment, and an ultrasound machine. An oversized billboard at the entrance displays the name of the clinic in bold letters—PRECISION ULTRASOUND CLINIC (Figure 5.1).

F I G U R E 5.1   Precision Ultrasound Clinic (© Sunil K. Khanna)

On my first visit I could not meet Dr. Verma. Madhu, the clinic receptionist in her mid-twenties, informed me that the doctor was out on a home visit. Madhu commuted to the clinic at least six days a week from her home in a residential settlement about six miles to the west of Shahargaon. Sensing my disappointment, she confided in me that the best time to meet the doctor was before 9:30 AM. I decided to request an appointment and arranged to revisit the clinic one week later. This time Madhu asked me to sit in the waiting room. I observed that Madhu was busy welcoming patients, checking their appointments, and asking them for relevant medical documents. Another woman was assisting her from behind the reception counter. I overheard Madhu sternly giving directions to the cleaning woman:

> You must make sure that you thoroughly clean the patient waiting room. Yesterday, the lady doctor got mad at me when she saw that the chairs in the room were not properly dusted. If you continue to work like this, I am afraid we both will lose our jobs. The doctor expects us to keep everything clean and up-do-date. She does not like trash strewn around in the patient waiting room.

The cleaning woman defended the quality of her work by saying that she was doing her best. At one point in their animated conversation, Madhu looked at me and apologized. She felt uncomfortable that I was witnessing this conversation. "The workers here, especially the cleaning people, have to be monitored regularly," she proclaimed in justifying her stern remarks. She continued:

> I keep telling everyone that we are competing for patients in this locality. There are other clinics providing maternity services. We serve our customers well by keeping our premises clean and professional looking. We provide the best medical services in the area and we take good care of our patients. Our customers will not object to paying for medial care. In fact, they will go and tell others about our clinic. This is the best way to advertise for our clinic.

Madhu's rationale appeared consistent with her work managing the front desk, serving as a spokesperson for the clinic, and maintaining a professional-looking reception area.

Dr. Verma arrived promptly at 9:30 AM, the time of our appointment. After a quick formal greeting she led me into her office, which was small and narrow with marble floors. The office furniture was arranged in a way to clearly demarcate the physician's space from that of the patient. A window allowed natural light through its panes. Two steel cabinets with glass stood against the wall behind the physician's desk. The cabinets held piles of paper organized in large legal-sized folders, notebooks, medical equipment, and a few hardbound books. The boldly printed titles on the book covers suggested that these were obstetrics and gynecology books. Our conversation quickly focused on the diagnostic facilities at the clinic. I asked

Dr. Verma about new reproductive technologies available in Shahargaon and specifically at her clinic. She pointed to a large, four-color poster on the wall and said:

> Unlike in the past, we now have access to the best prenatal diagnostic facilities here. Specifically, here at this clinic we can only do ultrasonography. There are several other clinics in the area that provide ultrasonography. We do not have any diagnostic center that provides other more sophisticated reproductive technologies. We really do not need such specialty services here.

The poster on the wall had hand-drawn pictures and flow diagrams of the various prenatal diagnostic techniques. I followed up with a quick question, "But what do these technologies diagnose?" I asked in anticipation of learning as much as I could about this topic. I felt fortunate to be interviewing a clinician who was willing to talk to me about her profession. She patiently explained:

> These techniques can tell us a lot about prenatal development and overall health of the fetus. We can learn if the fetus is growing normally or, during late pregnancy, if the fetus is positioned correctly for a normal vaginal delivery. The new reproductive technologies are especially useful in identifying major birth defects in the fetus. There is no doubt that these new technologies have been very useful in improving pregnancy outcomes. Previously we did not have these miracle technologies.

I was impressed with Dr. Verma's emphatic and frequent use of the word "miracle" during our conversation. She was the third doctor I interviewed who had used the term "miracle" to describe the new reproductive technologies. From the perspective of a medical provider, the new technologies are capable of visualizing and projecting the prenatal world in terms of identifiable patterns of normal fetal growth and fetal abnormalities. By helping physicians visualize the otherwise obscure intrauterine world, the new technologies have had a profound influence on the practice of medicine, especially in the area of obstetrics. Dr. Verma described how the Precision Ultrasound Clinic received its first ultrasound machine in 1992:

> In those days, the ultrasound machine was bulky and came with a number of accessory items like transformer, power storage, etc. I did not have enough money to buy the machine; so I leased it because I believed that women in the area will be helped by the use of the machine. In 1992, Precision Ultrasound Clinic was the only place where one could get ultrasonography. Over time other clinics also acquired ultrasound machines. At present, there are three more clinics in the area that provide

ultrasonography services. In the past, women had to travel to the government hospital for emergency care. Everyone knows that medical care at government hospitals is substandard because there are too many patients and too few doctors. However, women in this area do not need to use government hospitals for health care. They now have access to the best and most modern medical services. Here at this clinic we provide state-of-the-art health care by using the most modern ultrasonography machines. In my experience, the demand for ultrasonography has increased in this area. Some clients ask for an ultrasound exam when there is no medical need for it. I believe they want to know if they are pregnant with a girl. I refuse to perform such tests. I only perform ultrasound exams when there is a medical need like a pre-existing health condition or to simply monitoring pregnancy.

Our interview session was interrupted by numerous phone calls, by the receptionist wandering in and out of the doctor's office, and by the cleaning woman tidying up the office. "Can you tell the sex of the fetus by using ultrasonography?" I asked. "Well, not always. It depends on the timing of the ultrasonography exam and also on the position of the fetus." Her reply was more medical and clinical than I had expected. She continued:

Ultrasonography is now routinely performed. It is safe and reliable. It can confirm pregnancy at a very early stage say by eighth or tenth week of gestation. I think ultrasonography can tell the sex of the fetus by week twelve onwards. But I know there are some clinics that claim to identify the sex of the fetus around tenth week. I am not sure if that is accurate.

I asked a follow-up question: "Is there demand for ultrasonography?" "Oh yes, very much so. Parents come from all over the area including the neighboring villages and towns looking for ultrasonography tests. But you should know that since 1995 it is illegal to perform prenatal sex determination tests in India," Dr. Verma responded excitedly. "But why do they want these tests?" I asked. My question evoked a mixed response. Dr. Verma was slightly uncomfortable but answered nonetheless:

You are an Indian and you know that in our society parents prefer boys over girls. I think that is why parents want this test so that they can tell if they are going to have a boy or a girl. But I must tell you that some parents simply want this test because that is what their doctor has recommended. So that you know, ultrasonography is not serving just one purpose. In my practice, I get about five to ten cases per week out of twenty-five to thirty cases total, of parents seeking ultrasonography simply to know the sex of the fetus.

"Do you tell them the sex of the fetus?" I asked. "Actually no, I do not." She then responded emphatically:

First, I personally do not think it is appropriate for me to tell them the sex of fetus. I am a woman and I know how hard it was for me to become a doctor. I was raised in a family where my parents expected their sons to succeed and become doctors and engineers. Although our parents educated their daughters, they expected us to become school teachers or simply educated housewives. I do not think when my parents sent me to school they were thinking that someday I will become a doctor and run my own clinic. Having experienced discrimination at home, in medical college, and even in my profession, I strongly feel the need to improve the status of women in our society. You can say it is a personal issue for me. That is why I do not want to tell my patients the sex of the fetus, especially if it is a girl. Also, I know it is against the law. And finally there is the medical issue. I think in some cases I just cannot tell for sure if the fetus is a boy or a girl. It depends on the timing of the test and the position of the fetus.

I inquired if she knew about other clinicians in the area who shared her views against the use of ultrasonography for prenatal sex identification. Dr. Verma replied:

The truth of the matter is that some do misuse ultrasonography. A few doctors are in the business of making money not in the practice of medicine. Unfortunately those doctors are using this technology [ultrasonography] for the wrong purpose. It is not intended to use in this way. It is grossly unethical and illegal. I believe that ultrasonography is an excellent diagnostic technology. One must not stop using it simply because a few are manipulating it for identifying female fetuses. Those doctors should be prosecuted under the Prenatal Diagnostic Techniques Act. But one must be careful to not punish the technology or those who use it for appropriate purposes. Under no circumstances should our government restrict people's access to ultrasonography.

At the conclusion of our meeting, Dr. Verma advised that I consult relevant medical texts and learn about the science behind new "miracle technologies" now available in India. "You should study the science behind the new reproductive technologies before writing a social commentary on their use or misuse," she advised. I agreed that she had a point to make—many social researchers have been critical of the role of technology in controlling reproduction, but in their writing they often undermine their credibility by failing to describe the scientific underpinnings of these technologies. I left the clinic convinced that learning about the science of new reproductive technologies could help me develop a solid knowledge base for examining their use.

THE SCIENCE OF "MIRACLE" TECHNOLOGIES

I followed up on Dr. Verma's advice and went to the National Medical Library in New Delhi to pour over numerous books and articles on the scientific and technological aspects of new reproductive technologies. In my search I found that the label "new reproductive technologies" in medical literature refers medical technologies specifically used for prenatal imaging, *in utero* diagnosis of birth defects, and assisted reproduction. Although they are still referred to as "new", they were first developed in the 1960s as medical diagnostic tools for prenatal examination and treatment for infertility. Having made staggering advances in the past forty years, new reproductive technologies provide live and vivid images of the intrauterine world, and a broad range of reproductive choices. New reproductive technologies have now become a part of the routine medical care worldwide. Medical professionals, like Dr. Verma, regard these technologies as playing a vital role in improving women's health. New reproductive technologies fall into two categories—prenatal screening technologies (PST) and assisted reproductive technologies (ART).

Prenatal Screening Technologies (PST)

Prenatal screening technologies use imaging, genetic and biochemical testing to examine normal or abnormal development of the fetus and to monitor the progression of pregnancy. These technologies represent the cornerstone in providing medical care during pregnancy. The various technologies commonly include ultrasonography, amniocentesis, and chorionic villus sampling. They allow clinicians to diagnose birth defects, examine and monitor mother's health and fetal development, and perform intrauterine therapeutic intervention.

Ultrasonography is widely used in many branches of medicine, especially in obstetrics and gynecology. It sends out high frequency sound waves to create images of the body and internal organs. The technique is noninvasive and does not involve the collection of bodily fluid or tissue samples. In a routine prenatal exam, the ultrasound procedure takes ten to thirty minutes. The clinician rubs warm mineral oil or transmission gel over the woman's abdomen and slowly moves a transducer over the abdomen to obtain pictures, which can be copied or videotaped for later reference (Gorrie et al. 1998). Ultrasonography, now a standard procedure worldwide, provides information to confirm pregnancy, verify the location of the pregnancy, monitor fetal growth, identify fetal sex, and determine fetal age.

Amniocentesis involves using an aspiration needle to draw a small amount of amniotic fluid surrounding the fetus in the uterus. During pregnancy amniotic fluid serves as a medium of fluid exchange between the fetus and the mother.

Microscopic and biochemical analysis of the amniotic fluid allows diagnosis of genetic abnormalities in the fetus. Amniocentesis is appropriate any time after the fifteenth week of gestation. The procedure takes about forty-five minutes and is a fairly safe way to diagnose fetal abnormalities, such as chromosomal damage, congenital birth defects, and fetal anemia. The technique also reveals the sex of the fetus, with results available within a few days of sample collection (Malarkey and McMorrow 2000).

Chorionic villus sampling during the first trimester can help in the prenatal diagnosis of some genetic abnormalities, and is especially valuable in cases of high risk pregnancies. The criteria for recommending the use of chorionic villus sampling include mother's age above 35 years, a history of a previous fetus with anomalies, or couples who are carriers of genetic defects. The procedure involves taking a small tissue sample from the end of one or more chorionic villi, the hair-like projections of the membrane that surround the embryo. The clinician then microscopically examines the sample and tests for biochemical disease markers. This test is valid as early as the twelfth week of gestation, with quick results available within forty-eight hours. Although the procedure is generally safe, it carries the risk of a slight chance (less than 1%) of pregnancy loss (Gorrie et al. 1998).

Assisted Reproductive Technologies (ART)

Assisted reproductive technologies include medical tests and procedures for diagnosing and treating infertility. One of the most commonly used assisted reproductive technologies is called "in-vitro fertilization" or IVF. It involves several complex procedures—extracting a woman's eggs, fertilizing the eggs in the laboratory, and then transferring the resulting embryo into the woman's uterus. In-vitro fertilization allows for the selection of embryos free from genetic abnormalities. Although not defined as an intended purpose of this technique, sex selection is possible as part of the procedure. Sex chromosomes carried by sperm determine the sex of the fetus. Separation of X and Y bearing sperm and fertilizing the egg with the "desired" sperm produces a female or male fetus on demand. Since this technique is expensive, it is offered only by a few clinics in India.

RECONCEPTUALIZING "MIRACLE" TECHNOLOGIES

Since the 1980s ethical and social issues relating to the availability and use of new reproductive technologies in many societies have been hotly debated by academic, policy, and activist groups. Experts from diverse disciplinary backgrounds and expertise have expressed their views on issues as complex as the beginning of life, rights of the embryo and fetus, parenthood, motherhood, and the very meaning of kinship as redefined by the promises of new reproductive technologies (Edwards et al. 1999; Roberts 2006; Stanworth 1987; Strathern 1992). Notwithstanding considerable variability in perspectives and opinions, most agree that new reproductive technologies have raised complex ethical issues regarding rights of the embryo (Becker 2000). Some argue that conception, pregnancy, and birth are natural events and that the increasing reliance of medical practitioners on new reproductive technologies has led to an overly medicalized understanding of these natural events (Davis-Floyd and Sargent 1997; Ginsburg and Rapp 1995). Such "authoritative knowledge" promotes a techno-centric view of reproductive events preferred by biomedical practitioners, as it impersonalizes birth and marginalizes traditional healers and midwives.

Others observe that such medical technologies have become a "growth industry" attracting financial investment worldwide (Gupta 2000). Although widely available, these technologies have become very expensive, especially assisted reproduction technologies. In her study among couples seeking treatment for infertility in the United States, Becker (2000) points out that

> practitioners have flocked to new technologies aimed at the middle and upper classes. The actual cost of new reproductive technologies to the consumer is determined by several factors: the expense of operating a program and its laboratory, the labor involved in the procedures themselves, and the availability, or lack, of insurance to underwrite the cost. The median cost of a single cycle of IVF [in vitro fertilization] is now approximately $10,000; the incorporation of donor egg technology adds $5,000 or more to cost of a cycle. Costs have escalated as complex technical variations have proliferated. New reproductive technologies are now estimated to be a $350-million-a year business (Becker 2000: 13-14).

Worldwide, couples seeking the use of new reproductive technologies now have many choices. But the availability and use of these technologies necessitates a reinterpretation of all aspects of human reproduction, especially those associated with conception and birth. New reproductive technologies are redefining the very notion of what it means to be a person and what it means to have reproductive rights and choices. People's proclivity to make certain choices shows considerable variation and is embedded in culture. Thus, we must examine this phenomenon from a culturally relativistic perspective.[3]

In 1980, a clinic based study in India reported that the combined use of ultrasonography, amniocentesis, and female-selective abortion was related to son preference (Ramanamma and Bambawale 1980). A 1984 report brought national attention to the issue of sex-selective abortion, stating that from 1978 to 1983 nearly 78,000 female fetuses identified through prenatal sex determination technologies had been aborted in India (Parikh 1990). Early advertising during this period by profit-seeking enterprises emphasized the ability to identify the sex of the fetus more than the medical uses of the new technologies. Advertisements for prenatal sex determination technologies intensified throughout the 1980s and the

---

3. The term cultural relativism, one of the key concepts in anthropology, refers to understanding beliefs and practices of a group of individuals relative to their own cultural context. It cautions anthropologists against passing judgment on other people's beliefs and practices.

early 1990s. Private investment companies and business groups saw enormous financial potential in catering to the cultural preferences of the general public. Media campaigns specifically promoted ultrasonography as a reliable means for identifying the sex of the fetus or for offering "reproductive options" to married couples (Figure 5.2).

F I G U R E 5.2   Advertisements in regional and national newspapers (1993–1997) for diagnostic services, including ultrasonography, chorionic villus sampling, and amniocentesis for prenatal sex identification (© Sunil K. Khanna)

Billboards and newspaper advertisements cleverly promoted the economic benefits of using ultrasonography as an effective means of saving money by getting rid of unwanted female fetuses. This culturally based meaning and use of ultrasonography made it marketable. The one-time cost of using ultrasonography was justified as a small financial investment that the Indian couple must make in order to later save the cost of paying a dowry. The scientific innovation and rigor involved in the development and standardization of ultrasonography apparently did not involve a careful examination of the powerful cultural and market forces that would reshape its potential use. The most important questions are not about the technology itself, but rather about its relationship to cultural history and the contemporary capitalist economy.

How can a society use new reproductive technologies in a responsible and sensitive manner? Who should have access to these technologies and who should not? What should be the ethical principles guiding their use? How can society avoid their "misuse," or for that matter, what constitutes the "misuse"?

ULTRASONOGRAPHY IN SHAHARGAON

In this section I provide ethnographic information about the contrasting views regarding the knowledge and use of ultrasonography among married couples in Shahargaon. The following discussion points out salient differences between the "public" and the "scientific" or "biomedical" views on ultrasonography. The rationale for developing and testing the new reproductive technologies under controlled conditions in the laboratory is one thing; ensuring their responsible use for intended medical purposes in the wider world is another. Although medical professionals label these technologies as "neutral" scientific innovations promising to cure infertility and offer reproductive choices, their use in the public domain, as in the case of Shahargaon, has been far from neutral. Married Jat couples interpret the meanings and purposes of the technologies that doctors call "miraculous" to fit their own needs and everyday experiences.

One consequence of Shahargaon's urban assimilation has been the easy availability of "modern" medical facilities providing a range of health care services including primary care, ultrasonography, and abortion services. Among married Jat couples, ultrasonography is in popular demand as the preferred medical technology to identify the sex of a fetus during the early stages of pregnancy. In stark contrast with the past, the newly prosperous Jat families in Shahargaon find that ultrasound scans are not only easily accessible but also affordable. The cost of an ultrasound scan in the nearby clinics varies between $30 and $70 depending upon the reputation of the clinic and the type of scanning used. Married Jat couples are willing to pay for the procedure if it helps create a family of desired size and sex composition. They justify using ultrasonography and female-selective abortion as a two-step process to plan for a small family with the preferred composition. According to Megha, a 27-year-old married Jat woman, "Using ultrasound [ultrasonography] is a small investment to ensure long-term prosperity and security of the family."

I interviewed eighteen married Jat women under 45 years of age, a group most likely to make decisions regarding the use of new reproductive technologies for prenatal sex identification. None of the women mentioned using amniocentesis or chorionic villus sampling. They claimed little or no knowledge of these two prenatal diagnostic techniques. They all identified ultrasonography as the preferred technique for prenatal diagnosis. In their opinion, ultrasonography is a simple, noninvasive, affordable, and reliable medical procedure used to identify the sex of the fetus early in pregnancy. The women were knowledgeable about the availability and cost of ultrasonography, and they were familiar with medical facilities in the area where ultrasonography was available. They used Hindi-language words to describe the characteristics and purposes of ultrasonography. For example, they often referred to ultrasonography as "ultrasound" and ultrasonography equipment as "foreign-made" (*firangi*) X-ray machines or cameras—a label that acknowledges the western antecedents of ultrasonography, as well as its higher level of reliability in comparison to locally made X-ray machines.

Shobha, a 32-year-old Jat housewife and the mother of one girl and two boys, used ultrasonography during her second pregnancy because her first child was a girl. "I did not want another daughter. So I went for ultrasound," she remarked. She further elaborated on her experience of using ultrasonography at one of the local clinics:

> The lady-doctor had asked me to come to the clinic at 10 AM. Since my husband had to work that day, I went with my elder sister-in-law. I did not want to delay anymore because I was already almost three months pregnant. We walked to the clinic; it is only fifteen minutes from here. We waited for half-an-hour to see the doctor. She took me to a room inside the clinic for ultrasound. She used a small machine to touch my belly; the machine felt cold. Since it was a hot day, it felt nice. The doctor did not talk during the procedure. I kept praying please god make this baby a boy. I did not want to make the decision to abort if I was pregnant with a girl, but I knew I had to because I just could not have two daughters. I needed a son, so I kept praying throughout the procedure. The doctor took a long time; she was very nice to me and kept telling me to relax. Once she completed taking the pictures she asked me to wait outside her office. After about twenty minutes she called us into her office to tell us about the results of the ultrasound [ultrasonography]. We paid attention to every word the doctor spoke. She told us that there was nothing to worry about because everything looked normal. We looked at each other and asked the doctor if it was good news. The doctor said that we should plan for a big feast. Although the doctor did not tell me

whether I was going to have a son or a daughter, I knew that I was pregnant with a son.

Although deemed illegal under the Prenatal Diagnostic Techniques Act (PDTA), clinicians often use such indirect means to convey the sex of the fetus to the expectant mother or accompanying relatives. Sometimes the results of the ultrasonography exams are communicated to the mother by clinic staff other than the doctor. They also communicate information about fetal sex to the pregnant women in a way that cannot serve as evidence of a violation of the Prenatal Diagnostic Techniques Act.

Informed by her own experience, Shobha plays the role of an advisor or mentor to other women in the village who have questions regarding ultrasonography. She stated that ultrasonography is a "diagnostic procedure (*janch ka tareeka*) in which the doctor uses a foreign-made machine (*firangi*) for taking several pictures of the womb (*garbha*). These pictures can identify if the woman is pregnant with a boy or girl." Shobha's words effectively capture the prevailing views on ultrasonography among women in the village. Married Jat women show a high level of awareness about the availability and use of ultrasonography. They all identified prenatal sex identification as the sole purpose of ultrasonography, having learned about ultrasonography from other women in the village.

Since advertising for ultrasonography for the purpose of prenatal sex determination has been illegal since 1994, information about ultrasonography spreads by word of mouth from women who have used the procedure or claim to know about its use. Women not only act as carriers of information, but also as advisors to others who may want to use ultrasonography. Premlata, a 34-year-old Jat woman, describes how she learned about ultrasonography:

> I had heard about doctors using a medical camera [ultrasonography] in government hospitals, but I did now know that ultrasound was available in private clinics. Roshni told me that I could use it if I did not want a girl or to learn if I was pregnant with a boy. When I was pregnant, I did not want to know the sex of the baby. God has given me two boys and I am very happy. I know that this new camera can tell the sex of the baby before birth, but I do not think I will ever need it because I have two boys. I do not want any more children. I do not think it is wise for women to know about the sex of the baby before the baby is born. God wants us to know his wishes only when he delivers the baby in the arms of the mother.

Upon further questioning, Premlata agreed that women who have given birth to a daughter should use the camera if they want to avoid the birth of another daughter. Other Jat women also echoed the same sentiment that the use of ultrasonography should be limited to avoiding the birth of an unwanted second or third daughter. Most women do not support the use of ultrasonography during a woman's first pregnancy. They also associate ultrasonography with the practice of female-selective abortion. In their opinion, realizing son preference or avoiding the birth of an unwanted daughter is a two-step process. First, a woman has to use ultrasonography to identify the sex of the fetus and then, if needed, seek female-selective abortion. Women with close social ties also share information in casual conversations about the appropriate timing for an ultrasound scan and suitable ultrasonography clinics where doctors willingly disclose information about the sex of the fetus. Jat women learn about the cost, the timing, and the appropriate facilities they should visit if they want to use ultrasonography.

Most Jat men in Shahargaon, regardless of their age, were reluctant to talk about ultrasonography. Discussions about pregnancy-related issues, especially ultrasonography, occur mostly among women. Men are not directly involved in these discussions and often avoided my questions on this topic, or answered in a dismissive manner. I persisted in my questioning of Sant Raj, a 30-year-old Jat man, who finally relented:

> It is unbelievable to think that scientists have now created a machine that can tell you if the woman is pregnant with a boy or girl. During my mother's time, the village midwife (*dai*) or other elderly women in the house used to predict the sex of the unborn child. But they were mostly guessing. I do not think they were serious. No one even considered ending a pregnancy based on their predictions. Now things have changed. We have this amazing foreign machine and it always tells the truth. Families in Shahargaon take the results of ultrasound seriously. I do know about several cases of where a family has aborted a girl fetus based on the results of ultrasound.

In an interview with Yogesh, a 35-year-old Jat man, I asked what he knew about ultrasonography. Reluctantly, he expressed his opinion:

> Ultrasonography is used by pregnant women and pregnancy related matters are women's concerns. Jat men are not interested in women's issues. It is not appropriate for a man to ask his wife or women relatives in the house questions about conception, pregnancy, and childbirth. These are women's issues and they should deal with them. I don't think men in this village will be able to tell you anything important about ultrasound. For married couples in Shahargaon, ultrasonography serves only one purpose; that is, to identify the sex of the fetus during the prenatal period.

This culturally reinterpreted purpose of ultrasonography is in stark contrast to the broad benefits, as described in medical textbooks, of the diagnostic technique for preventing birth defects and improving birth outcomes for women and children.

"MISUSE" OR "CHOICE"

Many scholars, activists, women's groups, and voluntary agencies condemn pre-natal sex determination and female-selective abortion as a "blatant misuse" of ultrasonography to discriminate against the unborn girl (Gupta 1991; Patel 1989). They argue that female feticide is a manifestation of the same patriarchal ideology that results in a strong preference for sons and disfavor for daughters. They suggest that female feticide, if unchecked, might result in a significant deficit of women by seriously unbalancing India's sex ratio (Gillis, 1995; Luthra 1993; Miller 2001; Wertz and Fletcher 1989).

In opposition to the prevailing viewpoint among professionals, some policy makers and members of the medical community believe that it provides re-productive "choices" for women and may serve as an effective means of reducing family size. This minority voice promotes ultrasonography as an important tool in the promotion of population control programs and as a possible "solution" to India's population problem (Balasubrahmanyan 1986). Some doctors who run clinics in Shahargaon strongly favor this position and oppose any regulation of ultrasonography by the Indian government. Meanwhile, married couples in Shahargaon are harnessing the power of ultrasonography to respond to the pres-sures of an urban lifestyle by limiting family size and acting upon preexisting cultural beliefs associated with son preference. They justify the importance of prenatal knowledge in terms of its benefits in family planning and in response to the everyday struggles for survival, long-term financial security, and adaptability to the urban environment of New Delhi. They describe raising daughters as full of anxiety and "tension" linked to the fear of sexual indiscretion on part of the daughter in the "corrupt and dangerous" urban world. They describe sons as "socially immune" to the vices of the city. The motivations of Jat women derive from individual as-pirations, demands by spouses and other family members, and by the larger worldview of the village community. The use of ultrasonography as part of a family-building strategy has reinforced Jat women's roles as reproducers, empha-sizing their ability to meet a strong cultural expectation and contribute sons to their husband's lineage. The sanctity of childbirth, at least in this context, is secondary to a woman's ability to give birth to a son.

In spite of the culturally conditioned views of the user of ultrasonography in Shahargaon, local medical practitioners continue to describe ultrasonography exclusively in the glowing terms of a "miracle" technology that improves the out-comes of pregnancy. Such idealistic constructions contribute to maintaining a façade of non-participation in the use of ultrasonography for prenatal sex determination. Doctors conveniently ignore abundant evidence both in their practice and in the literature suggesting that the use of these technologies most often does not conform to the intended medical purposes (Gupta 2000; Jeffery et al. 1984; Khanna 1997; Sudha and Rajan 1999).

For Shahargaon Jats, ultrasonography carries the prestige of western science and technological innovation. Their motives for using ultrasonography are grounded in their history and value system, everyday economic realities, and the desire to limit family size—not in the pronouncements of science.

Chapter 6

✳

Accessing Diagnostic and Abortion Services

In this chapter, Jat women's narratives provide an inside look at the traditional practice of prenatal sex identification which is still a recognized area of expertise for the village midwife and other elderly women. Narratives of younger women reveal how they use new technologies for prenatal sex identification in a different context and for a different purpose. I examine the influence of government family planning programs, difference in attitudes and behavior related to socioeconomic status, how pregnant women select clinics and doctors, under what circumstances they feel the most pressure to find out the sex of the fetus and then seek sex-selective abortion, their apprehensions and experiences in the clinical setting, and the incidence of accidental male feticide. Women also talk about decision making within the family and their own preferences and feelings, including both compliance and resistance.

TRADITIONAL KNOWLEDGE AND PRENATAL SEX IDENTIFICATION

My interview with Pyari, the village midwife, was interrupted by a knock at the door. A man whispered, "Pyari, are you at home? My wife has started experiencing labor pain. My mother thinks it is time for you to come." Without moving or looking at the door, Pyari hurled a loud question the man, "Are you sure it is labor pain?" "How would I know? Mother told me to bring you. So I am here. Please come with me and examine my wife," the man tensely replied. Pyari frowned and dropped her cup of tea onto her plate with a clatter. "Look at my life. Even in this old age I am working all the time. It is almost midnight and I need some sleep. But now I have to go and take care of my second childbirth of the day." Pyari did not direct her comments at anyone in particular. She simply expressed her exasperation with the fact that no woman in her extended family, especially her daughter-in-law, was interested in becoming a midwife. She lamented not being able to pass on her knowledge and experience.

Pyari is the only traditional midwife in Shahargaon, a village whose members now have easy access to modern medical care facilities. Pyari lives with her husband in a well-built single-story house in the village. Pyari's family, including two sons, two daughters-in-law, and four grandchildren, live in a two-story house next door. As an experienced midwife and elderly woman, Pyari is respected by everyone in the Jat community. Her husband, Prabhu Ram, works at the local government hospital, which further adds to Pyari's status. Jat families often seek medical advice and help from both Pyari and Prabhu Ram. Pyari belongs to the Harijan caste, which ranks low in the social hierarchy of the village. According to Pyari:

> Not long ago, Jats in this village used to call us untouchable (*achut*) or sweeper (*churha*). They do not use those derogatory terms anymore because now the world has changed. Shahargaon is now an urban village. Also, several members of my caste have jobs and they are no longer collecting garbage from Jat homes. A few Harijan families in this village are as affluent as Jat families. Our men have found jobs in government offices and our children now go to English-medium schools.

The term "sweeper" (*churha*) refers to their traditional occupation. The term "untouchable" (*achut*) symbolizes the state of "impurity or pollution" ascribed to the members of Pyari's group because of their traditional occupation. Since the 1970s, several Harijan families in Shahargaon have taken advantage of the growing real estate market by selling and renting portions of their residential property. Harijan men work as traders, street vendors, construction workers, and drivers in the surrounding urban milieu. Pyari's two sons have been especially successful in establishing a real estate business.

I wanted to accompany Pyari on her trip to her client's house. But sensing the tension in her voice, I could not muster up enough courage to ask for permission. Pyrai got ready in a hurry. She gave me a tense look and said, "What are you doing? Get ready, you are coming with me. We can finish our conversation on the way to my client's house." Playing the role of an obedient anthropologist and feeling somewhat desperate for field data, I followed her out of the house and walked with her through the narrow lanes in the village. During our short walk, we talked about many issues, including inter-caste relations, traditional childbirth practices, and son preference in Shahargaon. Pyari spoke with a commanding voice clearly audible even amidst the distant but loud sound of barking dogs.

Pyari boasted to me that she could predict the sex of the fetus only by looking at the mother:

> I can tell the sex of the fetus by observing the mother's walk and the way she lies down. I can tell it because I have seen so many pregnant women and have delivered so many babies. But Jat families do not believe me

when I say that the woman is pregnant with a girl. They will always find something wrong with my prediction. I know it is because they all want to hear the good news. They all want to hear that it is going to be a boy and not a girl.

According to Pyari, Shahargaon Jat families have always shown a strong preference for sons over daughters. It is not a new phenomenon:

Son preference in this village is as old as the village itself. I remember when I started delivering babies in this village, Jat mothers-in-law would always tell me, 'Pyari, make sure that the child you deliver is a boy. We already have too many girls. I want to see the face of a grandson (*pote ka muh dekhun*).' I used to tell them that the sex of the baby is not in my control. It is always determined by god and fate. Whatever god has made inside the mother's womb is what will be born. I cannot change a girl into a boy. I can only deliver a baby and make sure both the mother and the baby are okay. I have been working as a midwife in Shahargaon since it became a real village, and I have never heard any woman tell me that she wants to give birth to a daughter. They all want sons.

Pyari's comments point to a long enduring tradition of son preference that continues to define the community even today. In spite of the urban assimilation of the village, conception and pregnancy are events that trigger significant anxiety and speculation. Women nervously wait to learn about the prediction of the sex of the fetus made by the village midwife or elderly women in their neighborhood. Pyari uses a variety of methods—timing of conception, changes in the body of the pregnant woman, or her food preferences—to predict the sex of the fetus. A woman usually conceives a son during the waning phase of the moon and a daughter in the waxing phase of the moon. Elderly Jat women observe physical changes in a pregnant woman and her emotional state to make their prediction (Table 6.1). They even make inferences from the pregnant woman's dreams. Dreaming of a fruit or flower suggests that the woman is pregnant with a son. If she feels limited fetal movement, then she is carrying a daughter.

T A B L E 6.1   Indicators commonly used by Shahargaon Jat women to predict the sex of the fetus

Conception of a Daughter	Conception of a Son
Nipples turn black	Nipples do not change color
Fetus moves to the left side	Fetus moves to the right side
More belly bulge is visible	Less belly bulge is visible
Elongated belly bulge	Round belly bulge
Dark lines are visible on the belly	No dark lines are visible on the belly
Pregnant woman feels lethargic and tired	Pregnant woman feels active
Pregnant woman sleeps on her left side	Pregnant woman sleeps on her right side
Pregnant woman prefers mild food	Pregnant woman prefers spicy food

In a group interview with Jat women, I asked if they believed it was really possible to predict the sex of the fetus. They answered a loud "YES" citing several cases in which predictions were correct. However, more than focusing on the accuracy of their predictions, women enjoy speculating about the sex of the fetus. Typically when women relatives and neighbors learn about a pregnancy, they meet in the house of the pregnant woman to talk and make their predictions. Dharmo, a Jat woman in her sixties, described these meetings as "filled with laughter and fun." Jat men are never present; women sing and cook traditional food, reinforcing existing personal and family alliances, and establishing new relationships. Dharmo characterized these meetings as "women's moments." She continued:

> After hearing the news of pregnancy, we would gather at the home of the pregnant woman and congratulate the family, especially the mother-in-law. Experienced women would sit and make their predications if the child would be a boy or girl. In this village, there are still many women who can correctly predict the sex of the unborn child. We have learned from our mothers-in-law and they learned from their elders. It is our women's special knowledge and it is based on experience. I have correctly predicted the sex of all my grandchildren. I just know when and what to look for in a pregnant woman.

Dharmo's most vocal supporter in the group was Sushila, a Jat woman in her forties. Sushila has three children—two boys and a girl. She exclaimed, "Dharmo has never been wrong. She has correctly predicted the outcome of all my pregnancies. I have been pregnant three times. By the fourth or fifth month of the pregnancy, Dharmo could tell me if I was going to have a boy or a girl." I was surprised to find that every woman in the group agreed that Dharmo and a few other women in the village could correctly predict the sex of the unborn child.

A pregnant woman and her family express joy and happiness if the prediction is about the conception of a son. In contrast, if the prediction is about the conception of a daughter, their response is unenthusiastic. Nevertheless, I did not hear about any case of induced abortion of a suspected female fetus based on such traditional prenatal predictions. Jat women emphatically denied any knowledge of female-selective abortion either in the past or the present. According to Sushila:

> Although women lose many conceptions or their "conceptions fall" (*garbh girna*) for one reason or another, they never choose induced abortion if the traditional prenatal prediction indicates the conception of a daughter. Even in the early days when women did not know about the medical camera [referring to ultrasonography], women in this village never considered abortion on this basis. Although women did not like giving birth to many daughters, they did not have to worry about keeping a small family. They did not mind having many children. In fact, they preferred to have six, seven, or even eight children with the hope

that they would help out in household and agricultural work. Also, these predictions are not meant to be taken very seriously. They are simply predictions; they can be right or wrong. It is all fun and not all that serious. I think it is a good reason for women to meet and give advice to the pregnant woman regarding what to do and not do or what to eat and what to avoid.

Jat women are not secretive about their traditional knowledge related to prenatal sex determination. They openly share their knowledge with others, including family and nonfamily alike, and unhesitatingly make predictions regarding the sex of the fetus. In the past predictions about fetal sex by village women were public. Married couples never considered aborting a female fetus for several reasons. First, during their agricultural days, Jat couples showed a strong preference for sons, but did not consider large family size to be a problem. A large family was crucial in a labor-intensive agricultural economy. Consequently, Jat families had little reason to seek an abortion for a suspected female fetus. Second, in the pre-1970s period, married couples in Shahargaon had limited access to either temporary or permanent methods of contraception. Thus they did not have an effective means of preventing conception. Third, most indicators of prenatal sex identification used by village women are not noticeable until the second trimester of pregnancy. Risking a woman's life at this stage to avoid the birth of a suspected female fetus would have threatened the well-being of the family and the community at large. They did not expect a mother to endanger her life or future reproductive capability for the sake of aborting a suspected female fetus. Instead of practicing female-selective abortion, couples tried to build a large family in order to have as many sons as possible.

THE INFLUENCE OF FAMILY PLANNING PROGRAMS

Since the 1970s, changes in subsistence, exposure to an urban lifestyle, and easy access to affordable health care encouraged many Jat couples to use health care services provided at government-run clinics and hospitals. Health workers from the Primary Health Center, located in the nearby town of Mandi, routinely visited the village to educate married couples about family planning. These visits exposed the community to state-sponsored family planning programs advocating for small families. Health workers gave free condoms to married couples, counseled women on the use of intra-uterine device (IUD) and the benefits of child spacing, and offered cash incentives for married couples who elected to undergo sterilization.

Although initially resistant to these changes, Jat couples gradually reached a high level of acceptance for both temporary and permanent methods of contraception and a preference for small family size. Having improved their economic status, Jat families are now most likely to use private rather than publicly-funded health clinics, especially private clinics that provide prenatal care, as well as diagnostic, abortion, and children's services.

ATTITUDE AND BEHAVIOR DIFFERENCES BASED ON SOCIOECONOMIC STATUS

In 2003, I conducted a community survey among fifty-eight married Jat women, aged 45 years or less, across the three economic groups to inquire about their preferences for family size and composition, their use of ultrasonography, and whether or not they had resorted to female feticide during the past five years. I collected more extensive narrative information covering the past three years. Among the women surveyed, fourteen (24%) belonged to *Economic Group A*, twenty-eight (49%) belonged to *Economic Group B*, and sixteen (28%) belonged to *Economic Group C*. Briefly, women belonging to *Economic Group A* live in "affluent" households (average annual household income = $2,000 or more) and are formally educated. Women belong to *Economic Group B* live in middle-income group households (annual household income range = $1,000 to $2,000). Men from these households work for low-paying jobs as drivers or security guards and women, in general, have no education beyond the primary school level. Women belonging to *Economic Group C* live in "low" income group households (average annual income less than $1,000). Men from these households work either as part-time laborers or on small contract jobs related to construction business. Women are only informally educated. Key findings (Table 6.2) of the survey covering all three income groups are as follows:

1) Fifty-four (93%) reported that they had used ultrasonography at least once during pregnancy.

2) Four (7%) reported that they did not use ultrasonography during pregnancy.

3) Out of the fifty-four women who reported using ultrasonography,

   a) Forty-nine (91%) reported that they inquired and learned about the sex of the fetus during or after the ultrasonography exam.

T A B L E   6.2   Reported incidence of the use of ultrasonography and female-selective abortion in Shahargaon (2003 Survey)

	Economic Group A# (%)	Economic Group B# (%)	Economic Group C# (%)	Total
Survey participants (married Jat women)	14 (24)	28 (48)	16 (26)	58
Used ultrasonography	12 (22)	27 (54)	15 (28)	54
Did not inquire about fetal sex	5 (100)	0	0	5
Inquired about fetal sex	8 (15)	27 (55)	15 (30)	49
Underwent female-selective abortion	3 (11)	19 (69)	6 (20)	28
Did not undergo female-selective abortion	5 (24)	7 (33)	9 (43)	21

b) Five (9%) reported that they used ultrasonography during pregnancy but did not inquire or learn about the sex of the fetus.

4) Out of the forty-nine women who inquired and learned about the sex of the fetus during or after the ultrasonography exam,

a) Twenty-eight (57%) reported that they decided to seek an abortion based on the results of ultrasonography. In all cases, they wanted female-selective abortion.

b) Twenty-one (43%) reported that they decided not to have an abortion based on the results of ultrasonography. In all cases, these women learned that they were pregnant with a male fetus.

Survey results clearly show that between 1998 and 2003, Jat women chose to selectively abort only female fetuses. None reported ever aborting a male fetus identified by ultrasonography. The self-reported use of ultrasonography and female-selective abortion showed little variation among Jat women across the three economic groups. However, five women belonging to *Economic Group A* reported using ultrasonography during pregnancy but not for prenatal sex identification. Instead, they used ultrasonography upon the recommendation of their doctor as part of routine prenatal examination. This finding suggests that better educated women from wealthier families are less pressured by some preference and more likely to use ultrasonography for legitimate medical reasons.

All five women were formally educated up to the high school level and expressed a strong preference for a small and balanced family composition (one son and one daughter). All other women who participated in the survey expressed a strong preference for more sons than daughters and admitted to using ultrasonography to learn about the sex of fetus. Overall, the use of ultrasonography for prenatal sex identification is very high among women in *Economic Groups B* and *C*.

FINDING "PREFERRED" CLINICS AND DOCTORS

Through their informal networks in the village, Jat women learn about which clinics have doctors or the staff members likely to inform them about the sex of the fetus. Jat women who have gone to such clinics become acquainted with the doctor and clinic staff. Several women described a sense of confidence in the services offered at a particular clinic because of their personal experience and knowledge. They openly recommend these clinics to other women. Clearly, the word of mouth plays an important role the selection of the clinic. According to Sandhya, a Jat woman in her early thirties:

It is easy for a woman to find out if she is pregnant with a girl or boy. All she has to do is ask the doctor. Most doctors tell you about it. They charge you some money for it, but they rarely say NO. I have heard about a lady-doctor at a local clinic. She does not give you any information. So women do not go to her clinic for ultrasound [ultrasonography]. But I know of other doctors who tell you if you ask them nicely. Sometimes they tell you that the news is good. And if they do not say anything or make a bad face, you know that it is a girl and not a boy. You have to be alert and pay attention to what the doctor is saying and doing.

Sandhya's statement captures one of the typical ways in which Jat women interact with doctors performing ultrasonography. Shano, a Jat woman in her late twenties, describes how she learned from a doctor that she was pregnant with a son:

> When I got pregnant for the second time my friend in the village told me to go to a clinic in Mandi for ultrasound [ultrasonography]. She advised me that I should politely ask the doctor about the sex of the baby. It was important for me to know the sex this time. I already had a daughter. I wanted my second child to be a son. I did not want to go to just any clinic. I have heard of a case where a doctor scolded a woman for inquiring about the sex of the baby. The doctor told her that it was immoral and illegal. I did not want to pay for an ultrasound [ultrasonography] if they were not going to tell me what I wanted to know. So my husband and I went to the clinic in Mandi. After the ultrasound [ultrasonography] test, I politely asked the doctor. At first she did not say anything. Later when I was getting ready to leave, she smiled and told me that it was good news and that I should be very happy. I thanked the doctor. My husband was so happy that he gave extra money and a box of sweets to the receptionist at the clinic.

Shano's experience is typical of how Jat women identify and patronize diagnostic clinics where doctors of staff members are amenable to giving information about the sex of the fetus.

Sometimes a doctor or a clinic employee requires an additional fee to reveal the sex of the fetus. Women do not mind paying more money as long as they feel confident about receiving reliable results. They regard paying higher fees as an indicator of reliability. Kalyani, a 30-year-old Jat woman, told me that she is personally acquainted with an assistant to the doctor at a local ultrasonography clinic. The assistant discloses test results for an additional fee. Kalyani explained:

> My mother-in-law and I went to a nearby clinic. We knew the receptionist at the clinic. When the doctor was doing my ultrasound [ultrasonography] exam, I asked her if it was a boy or a girl. She refused to tell me and was angry at me for asking such a question. She told me that it was illegal. I was sad because I already have two daughters. I wanted a son. Afterwards the receptionist told me to come later in the evening if I wanted to know the results of the test. She also told me to bring some more money. So, I went back and paid her additional money. I do not

mind paying more money as long as I can trust the results. I know the doctor at this clinic was very good; she charges twice as much as what they charge at other clinics in the area. I paid the receptionist the money. She told me that I should be happy with the results because this time I did not have to worry about getting an abortion.

Women's narratives also showcase common strategies they use to seek information on fetal sex. They might directly ask the doctor or the assistant; pay attention to the indirect words, body language, and gestures of the physician; or pay extra money. Son preference is so strong in Shahargaon that Jat women use any means necessary to learn the sex of the fetus during or after an ultrasonography exam.

RELIABILITY QUESTIONED AND RECHECKED

During interviews with clinicians, I found that sometimes they make mistakes in reporting the results of prenatal sex identification tests to their clients. The accuracy of ultrasonography depends entirely on the timing of the scan and the position of the fetus during the scan; it is not foolproof. The tendency in some diagnostic centers is to report a higher number of female fetuses than male fetuses to their clients. This distortion is consistent with the survey results above where 57% of the women were diagnosed with a female fetus. When ambiguity exists in prenatal sex identification, clinicians may report a fetus as female rather than male because they do not want to be held accountable for diagnosing a male when the woman is actually pregnant with a female. A doctor who runs a diagnostic center in Mandi explained:

> When the married couples are expecting the birth of a son on the basis of the ultrasound report, they are very unhappy to get the news that they have a daughter. They get mad and then they come and get mad at the clinic staff and often spread rumors about the poor quality of services provided by the clinic. So, one has to be precise in reporting the results of an ultrasound exam, especially when it is about sex identification.

At some diagnostic centers practicing physicians have established financial arrangements with clinics that provide abortion services. These arrangements involve diagnostic centers receiving an established kickback fee, usually up to 10% of the cost of the procedure, for referring women seeking abortions. This network of reciprocity ensures a steady flow of clients seeking services from diagnostic clinics to abortion centers.

Double-ultrasonography is an emergent trend in Shahargaon. It involves two ultrasound examinations—the first to identify the sex of the fetus and second to confirm the findings of the first examination. Some women reported that they prefer to use two ultrasound exams from two different clinics to be certain that they do not abort a male fetus by mistake. They point to two recent cases in the village in which women were misdiagnosed as carrying a female fetus. Based on the results of their ultrasound exams, both women chose abortion only to learn that they were pregnant with male fetuses. Although I was unable to confirm the identity of the misdiagnosed women or how they came to know the sex of the fetus after the abortion, their cases are object lessons about the need for a second opinion for other women in the village. The use of ultrasonography exclusively for the purpose of prenatal sex determination is fraught with ambiguities and distortions.

MALE FETICIDE

Since 1993, when I first started working in Shahargaon, I have never heard of a single case of planned male-selective abortion in the village. When I asked about the incidence of male feticide, my informants dismissed it as an absurd idea. Sushila expressed her views as follows:

> Why would we even consider aborting a boy? We want boys. Everyone in this village wants at least one boy. Most want two boys. People here use ultrasonography to learn if they are pregnant with a girl. We worry about having too many girls. We are not concerned about having too many boys. We want too many boys. It is unthinkable for a woman to go for abortion after she learns that she is pregnant with a son. Anyone who does that must be crazy (*pagal*).

In one unique but interesting case, the abortion of a male fetus misdiagnosed as a female fetus, was averted because of general family pressure against abortion. Shano described this case:

> Right in this village it happened just a year ago. I cannot tell you the name of the woman or the family. But the instance is very interesting. We all talk about it. A Jat woman who already had two daughters learned that she was pregnant again. She desperately hoped that this time she would deliver a boy. Her family members, including her husband and mother-in-law, all wanted a son. So they all agreed to for an ultrasound [ultrasonography]. The doctor told her that she was pregnant with a girl. Considering her strong desire to have a son, the pregnant woman decided to abort the fetus. The husband supported her decision, but the mother-in-law did not. The mother-in-law insisted that she should not abort the fetus because it would be morally wrong and against the will of the god. I also heard that there was some tension in their family over this issue. The woman reluctantly carried the fetus to term only to give birth to a boy. Everyone in the village was shocked to learn this. People did not know

how to react to the news. The woman and her family are very happy now and are relieved that she did not accidentally abort a boy.

In this case, the role of the mother-in-law and the decision not to seek sex-selective abortion underscore a situation in which religion and morality are barriers against sex-selective abortion. Although only a few women in the village doubt the reliability of ultrasonography in accurately identifying the sex of the fetus, it is often a point of contention among family members especially when this information is used to decide whether or not the woman should seek sex-selective abortion. This example also highlights the complex steps and negotiations involved not only in learning about the sex of the fetus, but also in reaching the decision to seek female-selective abortion.

APPROPRIATE TIMING FOR FETAL SEX IDENTIFICATION

For most accurate results, a pregnant woman should seek ultrasonography between the sixteenth and the twentieth week of pregnancy and the fetus should be positioned in a way to allow for sex determination (Witlow et al. 1999). Jat women carefully consider the timing and cost of ultrasonography. Most believe that the third or fourth month of pregnancy is the most appropriate period to identify the sex of the fetus through the use of ultrasonography. Megha, a 27-year-old married Jat woman, stated her opinion:

> I believe that for increased accuracy, ultrasound [ultrasonography] should be performed sometime during the fourth month. It is the best time to know the sex of the baby. The lady-doctor told me that at this stage the test is most reliable and if one needs an abortion, it can be done without much problem. I know some women in the village who do not want to wait for that long. They want ultrasound [ultrasonography] to be done at the beginning of the third month. I do not think they should do it. But I know some women in the village who have used ultrasound [ultrasonography] early in their pregnancy. I always tell them, this is serious business and they should do whatever it takes to get an accurate result.

> Ganeshi, a 35-year-old Jat woman, agrees with Megha: I think women should wait until the fourth month to get an ultrasound [ultrasonography] test. This way there is less chance of the doctor making a mistake. No woman wants to abort a boy by mistake. And doctors do make mistakes especially when they do the test in the third month. So if a woman wants a son, then she should wait for accurate results so that she does not have to do the test again and again.

Both women believe that seeking a late-term abortion poses financial and logistical problems. Late-term abortion costs more and takes longer than first-term abortion. After the procedure the woman needs to spend at least six to eight hours at the clinic for observation. Most women believe their long absence from home could present a problem in raising suspicion among family members or relatives who oppose late-term abortion. Notwithstanding the cost of diagnostic and abortion procedures and the health risks involved in undergoing repeated late-term abortions, Jat women still use this means as a reliable way to avoid the birth of an unwanted daughter.

LIMITATIONS OF SURVEY RESULTS

Despite my long-term fieldwork in Shahargaon, the possibility exists that the incidence of ultrasonography for prenatal sex identification and female-selective abortion is much higher than I am able to report here. Because of the personal nature of these topics, some Jat women were not willing to talk freely about their experiences. Despite my long term relationship with the Shahargaon community and repeated promises to keep my informants' views and information confidential, a host of cultural, generational, gender-related, and class factors prevented some women and men from participating in my study. In particular, some women were reluctant to share their views with my research informants or me because of the culturally problematic nature of women talking about reproductive issues with another person, especially a man.

Women in the under-thirty-five age group were more open than women in the over-thirty-five age group. Women in the *Economic Groups B* and *C* were more willing to talk than women in the *Economic Group A*. Most women in the latter group were concerned that their personal information might become public knowledge in the village and damage the prestige of their families. In some cases, women kept silent because they had used ultrasonography and underwent female-selective abortion without the knowledge of their mothers-in-law or other family members. In other cases, women who chose not to undergo female-selective abortion after ultrasonography often cited fears of social condemnation by other family members who were not likely to be supportive of the decision to abort or not to abort a known female fetus. In casual conversations, several women told me that they knew of someone else who had either aborted a female fetus or had successfully resisted pressure from family members to undergo female-selective abortion. They talked about female-selective abortion in general terms or used a third-person as opposed to a first-person style of narrative. I heard them utter such phrases as "female-selective abortion is very common in this village," or "everyone does it but not everyone talks about it," or "even I know several women who have used female-selective abortion many times." Although unconfirmed, I suspect that at least in some instances this supposedly second-hand information was true. I also suspect that some of these women, for all the reasons discussed above, may have reported their own experiences disguised as those of other women.

"QUICK AND EASY" ABORTION

Since the passage of the Medical Termination of Pregnancy Act (MTPA) in 1971, a woman in India can seek legal abortion if the pregnancy threatens her life or physical and mental well-being, or if there is substantial risk that the pregnancy will result in the birth of a newborn with a serious abnormality. The Medical Termination of Pregnancy Act also allows a woman to abort a pregnancy that may have resulted from a failure of contraception. Policy makers and others have described the Medical Termination of Pregnancy Act as a progressive step to provide women greater control over their reproductive lives and as an effective means to control population growth.

Several birthing centers and clinics in urban markets surrounding Shahargaon provide safe and affordable abortion services under the Medical Termination of Pregnancy Act. Doctors at these clinics commonly use either the vacuum aspiration (curettage) technique or the dilation and evacuation (D&E) technique for induced abortion. Doctors tend to use the vacuum aspiration or curettage technique for abortion up to the third month or early fourth month of pregnancy. According to Gorrie et al., the procedure involves dilating the cervix by:

> ...inserting a series of tapered metal rods that increase progressively in size. When the cervical canal is open, a plastic cannula is inserted into the uterine cavity. The contents are aspirated with negative pressure within approximately five minutes. Many health care providers then gently scrape the uterine cavity with a curette to ensure that the uterus is empty (Gorrie et al. 1998: 942).

Doctors use the dilation and evacuation technique for performing abortion during the fourth month of pregnancy. Although similar to the above in many ways, this technique requires considerable prior preparation involving the use of laminaria to dilate the cervix for twenty-four hours before abortion (Gorrie et al. 1998). Doctors consider both techniques to be safe and reliable. According to Dr. Anju Satija, an obstetrician who runs a maternity care clinic in the area, the selection of the technique depends entirely on the length of gestation:

> The vacuum aspiration technique is the most commonly used procedure here. This is because most women who come here for abortion are either in the third or early fourth month of pregnancy. Sometimes women do come here as early as the end of the second month and want to get an abortion. I rarely see women coming into this clinic for late-term abortions, especially after the fourth month. I do not perform late-term abortions here at this clinic because it requires prior preparation and post-operative care. I refer these cases to a nearby nursing home or government hospital. Those facilities are better equipped to handle late-term abortion cases.

Dr. Satija keeps meticulous records of her clients and, as required under the Medical Termination of Pregnancy Act, reports all abortions performed by her to the local health authorities. Before performing an abortion, she interviews the client and records her reproductive and medical history and inquires about the duration of her current pregnancy. During this pre-operative interview, Dr. Satija asks if her client knows the sex of the fetus or wants a female-selective abortion. Dr. Satija stated:

> I ask these questions because it is the only way for me to know if the woman knows the sex of the fetus. I tell her that by law I cannot perform a sex-selective abortion. I also ask her if she is choosing abortion under any pressure from her husband or parents-in-law. I have been practicing in this area for quite some time, but I have never heard a woman acknowledging that she knows the sex of the fetus or that she is being forced to terminate her pregnancy. They always say that they do not want any more children. Sometime I can tell that they are lying, but without any evidence I cannot turn them away. Women in this country have a legal right to terminate an unwanted pregnancy.

Dr. Satija's experience and opinions are shared by other doctors providing abortion services in the area. They describe their first priority as providing safe and reliable health care to their clients. Although many claim that they provide legal abortion services, they admit that they can never be too sure. Many admitted that women come to their clinics for abortion after having undergone ultrasonography for prenatal sex identification at another clinic. Under these circumstances, a woman can claim that her pregnancy is the result of failure of contraception, thus allowing the doctor to provide "legal" abortion services and deny any culpability in facilitating "illegal" female-selective abortion. If a woman does not volunteer the information on fetal sex, it is impossible for a physician to know if she is seeking a sex-selective abortion.

Jat women in Shahargaon describe the abortion services available in local clinics as a "quick and easy" (*jhatpat aur aasan*) means to end an unwanted pregnancy. During individual and group interviews, women frequently admitted to using abortion services. They reported that the abortion services available in the area were affordable and that they received caring treatment at the local clinics. However, a few women complained that doctors did not explain the abortion procedure, and that they were too afraid or nervous to ask any questions. Kalpana, a 30-year-old Jat woman, who sought two abortions between 2000 and 2002, told of her experience:

> When I went to the clinic, the lady doctor at the clinic did not talk to me. The nurse at the clinic asked me about my pregnancy. She filled out some forms and then took me to a room. No one talked to me or told me anything. In fact, I did not want to know what was going on at that time. I was anxious about the whole thing. I wanted to get over with it and get

out of the clinic. So, I did not ask any questions. I thought doctors know what they are doing and everything will be okay.

Women's preferences about going to certain clinics have little to do with their understanding of abortion procedures. Their decisions depend entirely on the accessibility, cost, and most importantly, the amount of time it takes to complete the procedure.

Women often face difficulty in arranging for ultrasonography and abortion services, especially when they feel pressure from family members who may feel strongly one way or another about their decision. They also make every effort to keep their actions a secret and prefer not to raise suspicion among neighbors or those who may not agree with their decisions. Another difficulty is in managing household work in their absence. To ease their burden, women seek counsel and support from like-minded women in their own household, supportive relatives in other households, or trusted friends living in the village.

BIRTH ORDER AND PRENATAL SEX IDENTIFICATION

A consensus exists among married couples about desired family size and sex composition. The most preferred family size and sex composition is a two-sons-one-daughter family. Jat couples make a conscious effort have at least one son. They never select against the birth of a second son, but express strong disfavor in case of the birth of a second daughter. Jat women tended to believe that it is appropriate for a married couple to seek selective abortion of female fetuses to avoid the birth of a second daughter. According to Satyavati, a 27-year-old Jat woman:

> A woman should not use ultrasound [ultrasonography] during her first pregnancy. She should let her fate decide whether she will give birth to a boy or girl. If she has a son, then she should not worry about the sex of the second child. Even if it is a daughter, she should be happy. Everyone should have at least one daughter in the family. In my opinion, ultra-sound [ultrasonography] should be used only when the woman already has one or two daughters and no son.

Thus, the sex of the living children strongly influences the decision to find out the sex of the fetus. Women are most likely to undergo ultrasonography for prenatal sex identification and sex-selective abortion of a female fetus if they already have a living daughter. If the married couple has a boy, they are less likely to use ultrasonography in the next pregnancy to identify the sex of the fetus. Jat couples almost never use ultrasonography for prenatal sex identification and sex-selective abortion in a random manner. Assuming preference for a three-child family, Jat couples would almost never use ultrasonography during the first pregnancy. If the first pregnancy results in the birth of a daughter, they are likely to use ultrasonography to identify the sex of the fetus during second pregnancy and, if necessary, use sex-selective abortion to avoid the birth of a second daughter. Unmet expectations for having a son may lead a couple to repeatedly use ultrasonography and female-selective abortion until they have achieved a desired family sex composition without increasing the number of children in their family. The availability and use of ultrasonography and abortion facilities have allowed married Jat couples a private means to fulfill their expectations for family size and sex composition of children as appropriate to the birth order of sons and daughters.

MANAGING SOCIAL AND PSYCHOLOGICAL PRESSURE

During my interview with Rajjo, a 35-year-old Jat woman, I commented that Jat women may be forced by their husbands and mothers-in-law to use ultrasonography and seek female-selective abortion. Rajjo responded:

> What you just said may not be true in all cases. In some cases women themselves want to know the sex of the baby before it is born. Sometimes it is the mother-in-law who forces her daughter-in-law to use ultra-sonography. Sometimes it is her husband. I even know of some cases where all family members, including the father-in-law, forced the woman to abort a girl.

Rajjo's comments reflect the circumstances of a majority of Jat women. Decision-making authority and processes change from household to household and from person to person. Jat women strongly believe that the decision to use ultrasonography and seek female-selective abortion should be made privately and collectively within the family. Given the emphasis on family in Shahargaon, this expectation is not surprising. Sometimes the pregnant woman either makes the decision alone or with the support of her husband. The husband typically acts as a second line of authority usually submitting to the authority of the mother-in-law. The husband supports the decision of his wife against the wishes of his mother only in rare instances. Most commonly, the mother-in-law, the husband, and the pregnant woman are involved in the decision-making process, and the mother-in-law usually plays a crucial role. Her authority almost always eclipses the wishes of the pregnant woman. In a typical scenario, the mother-in-law directly, or with the support of other family members, puts pressure on the pregnant woman to use ultrasonography for prenatal sex identification. According to Jugani Devi, a 64-year-old mother-in-law:

> When my daughter-in-law got pregnant for the second time, I told her that I wanted a grandson. She has already given me a granddaughter and this time it must be a boy. I told her that giving birth to a boy would be good for the entire family. I did not want to die without seeing the face

of my grandson. I told my daughter-in-law that she should go for an ultrasound [ultrasonography] and check if she is pregnant with a boy. If she is not pregnant with a boy then she should get an abortion (*safai karado*). My husband did not know about this, but my son did and he supported me. My daughter-in-law is very obedient; she comes from a respectable family in Haryana. So she agreed to my wishes. Fortunately, the doctor told us that my daughter-in-law is pregnant with a son.

Women who try and cannot produce sons are likely to become emotionally distraught over their compromised position within the family. Kasturi, a Jat woman in her late twenties, described her experience as follows:

In 2000 when I got pregnant, I already had a daughter. My mother-in-law was concerned that I might give birth to another daughter. She said that since I came from a family of three sisters, I could give birth only to girls. I did not understand why she said that, but I could sense that she did not want another granddaughter. I talked with my husband. He said that he was concerned about raising two daughters. I guess I realized that I did not have a choice. So, I went to an ultrasound center in Mandi. I went there with my husband. We had to pay some extra money to find out that the news was not good. I told my husband that I would only abort the child if he insisted on it. He said he wanted me to do it because he was sure we would have a son next time. So, I did. In 2002, I got pregnant again. The ultrasound showed that it was a girl. This time my husband did not say anything. So, I did not go for abortion. Now I have two daughters. My husband wants another child. He is sure next time it will be a boy. I am not so sure anymore. God wants me only to have girls. I think my mother-in-law is correct. A woman who comes from a family of girls and no boys can only give birth to girls. I will live the rest of my life as someone who has disappointed her husband and has not been able to bring happiness into the lives of her parents-in-law. I do not want any more children. I do not want to go through all that one more time. I just want to raise my two daughters. This is my fate.

Other Jat women in Shahargaon, just like Kasturi, feel intense family pressure to give birth to a son. They agree to undergo prenatal sex identification tests and female-selective abortion as a means to fulfill the expectations of their mothers-in-law and thereby, raise their status in their affinal homes. Women sometimes described their decision to use ultrasonography and undergo female-selective abortion as a necessary step to minimize conflict with other members of the family.

Not all mothers-in-law in Shahargaon forced their daughters-in-law to produce sons at any cost. In my interviews with Jat women, I learned about four cases where the mother-in-law did not support the decision of the married couple to seek prenatal sex identification and sex-selective abortion. This aberration in the role of the mother-in-law is described in by Rani, a 25-year-old Jat woman:

> After I got pregnant for the second time, my husband told me that this would be our last child and that he did not want any more children. He told me that he could not afford to have more children. I already had a daughter. Although my husband never said anything to me directly, I knew that he wanted a son. I went for an ultrasound and learned that I was pregnant with another daughter. I went for another ultrasound, just to confirm. The second ultrasound confirmed that I was indeed pregnant with a girl. I decided to go for an abortion. I was slightly over the third month pregnant. My mother-in-law did not want me to have an abortion. She resisted it and was angry. She did not speak with me for many days. But I was determined to have a son. She even tried to influence my husband, but he said he was not interested in the whole issue. He did not care about it. My husband's elder brother's wife (*jethani*) accompanied me to the clinic. We did not tell anyone about it. We said we are going to Mandi for shopping. We came back in the evening. I told my husband that I did not feel well and that I had some bleeding and maybe I had miscarried (*bacha girgaya*). He did not care much about it. After a year, I got pregnant again and I went for an ultrasound [ultrasonography]. I learned that I was pregnant with a boy.

The above-mentioned case exemplifies how Jat women show a tendency to internalize their own wishes and try to align their preference for family size and sex composition with that of their husbands and affinal relatives. A mother of sons is considered fortunate and powerful, while a mother of daughters, but no sons, is considered unfortunate (*abhagi*) and weak. Although some women in the village describe female-selective abortion as a sin that cannot be a justifiable act under any circumstances, it a heavy burden for a married couple to resist using ultrasonography and female-selective abortion. The power of the collective preference coupled with the everyday living circumstances of Shahargaon Jats have led to a reinterpretation of the government's slogan of "a small family is a happy family" (*chota parivar sukhi parivar*) as "a more sons, less daughters family is a happy family."

MORALITY AND RESISTANCE

Most Jat women in Shahargaon align their own choices with the expectations of their affinal relatives. However, the tendency toward internalizing the desires of her in-laws and willing compliance with these desires has exceptions. I spoke with several women who refused to undergo an ultrasonography exam or a female-selective abortion against the wishes of their mothers-in-law or husbands. Such resistance is sometimes met with retaliation and sometimes leads to emotional and physical abuse of both the mother and unwanted daughter. Fearing such retaliation and marginalization within the family, women reluctantly comply with the wishes of their husbands and mothers-in-law while maintaining internal resistance. Sandeshi, a 32-year-old Jat woman, described her painful experience:

> It is true that I could not say no to my family members. My husband, his father, his mother, and his brothers and their wives, they were all after me. My parents did not know about it and I think they too would have supported my husband. I could not talk to my parents. I guess I felt that I did not have a choice. I remember the night before the abortion. I was lying in my room; I did not feel well and I didn't want to talk to anyone. I cried all day long and ask for forgiveness from God (*Bhagwan*). That night was my daughter's last night. I fell asleep without eating. My daughter came to me in my dreams. I cried and asked for her forgiveness, and she forgave me. She said that I should not blame myself and that it is not my fault. I told her that I was helpless and I am unable to save her. It is very difficult for a mother to say that to her daughter. We promised each other that we would be together again as mother and daughter in our next lives. Yes, we promised and I intend to fulfill that promise. This year, my daughter would have been ten years old.

The family tension surrounding the decision to use ultrasonography and seek female-selective abortion is further heightened in situations where the pregnant woman's natal relatives get involved. The case of Sudha and Bhagwan provides an example of how a volatile domestic situation can arise when a woman refuses to comply with the family's wishes. Sudha and Bhagwan were married in 1991. Bhagwan and his brother own three shops in the Shahargaon market. He also runs a small cafeteria (*dhaba*) alongside the national highway. Two years after their marriage, Sudha gave birth to a daughter. A year later, when Sudha became pregnant again, Bhagwan and his mother insisted that she use ultrasonography to identify the sex of the fetus. They did not want another daughter. Reluctantly, Sudha complied. She did not want to argue with her husband. After the couple learned that Sudha was pregnant with a girl, Sudha told her husband that she wanted to continue the pregnancy. Her mother-in-law and husband disagreed. They told her that she must go for an abortion. Sudha and Bhagwan argued with each other and, at one point, Bhawan scolded her and blamed her for bringing pain and misery into his life. Sudha remained adamant that she would not "kill her daughter." This domestic discord resulted in considerable tension for Sudha. Bhagwan's family members threatened Sudha with physical harm if she did not choose to abort the fetus. After a heated altercation one day, Sudha, along with her daughter, left her husband's home. She went to Haryana to stay with her parents. When Sudha's parents learned about the situation, they were furious.

They decided not to send Sudha back to Shahargaon. After a month, Bhagwan went to Sudha's village to persuade her to return, but Sudha and her natal family refused to comply. She insisted on delivering the child in her natal village. Sudha's parents told Bhagwan that they supported their daughter's decision. Although enraged by her stance, Bhagwan relented and promised Sudha that he would treat her well and not force her to undergo an abortion. Sudha delayed her return to Shahargaon until she had delivered her baby girl.

Sudha described her experiences in terms of feeling isolated and fearing for her own safety and that of her daughter. Sudha's experience not only represents an exception to women's universal compliance with the expectations of their husbands and mothers-in-law, but also reveals the often hidden consequences of emotional abuse that women face if they decide to resist family pressure and refuse to abort a female fetus.

I found additional case of women's resistance in Shahargaon. Dhan Devi, a Jat woman in her mid-thirties, refused to go for an ultrasound exam claiming that she would never participate in this sin (*pap*). She adamantly exclaimed:

> I can never do it! I do not want to know if it is a boy or a girl. I can wait for nine months. My mother-in-law and sister-in-law were mad at me. My sister-in-law has two boys and I have two girls. They told me that I do not need any more daughters. I told them without daughters we cannot have sons. I argued with them and said that they too are women and they should not talk in this way. When my husband talked with me about it, I told him that he could find another wife because I am not going to commit this sin (*pap*). I refused to sleep in the same room. I even told my parents what was going on here. They were not happy about it and supported my decision. Everyone in the family was mad at me, but then they cannot force me to do it. After some time my mother-in-law gave up.

Sudha resisted aborting a female fetus citing moral conscience, and Dhan Devi equated abortion with sin and even refused to undergo an ultrasonography exam. Their stories reveal a moral basis for active resistance against authority in a patriarchal context. Both Sudha and Dhan Devi threatened to leave their husbands and both were supported by their natal relatives. Perhaps a feeling of isolation and a lack of support from her natal relatives led Sandeshi to resign herself to comply with the expectations of her affinal family.

The stories of the three women are in contrast to the academic discourse on female feticide that represents Indian women as helpless individuals lacking the ability to understand and express their own unique views, expectations, and aspirations. If preventing the "misuse" of ultrasonography and female feticide is the goal, then it is in these cases that I see potential for activism and change at the community level. One progressive change, i.e. small families, under certain circumstances may not produce another progressive change, i.e. balance in sex preferences for children. However, the seeds of resistance to prevailing norms of family-building practices may provide a foundation and rationale for future change.

Chapter 7

✳

Legal Regulation

In the early 1980s, the *Economic and Political Weekly*—one of the leading forums for debates and critical inquiry in India—published a series of articles on the use of ultrasonography for prenatal sex identification and the practice of female feticide. These publications sparked a contentious debate among scholars, journalists, and activists on the use of ultrasonography to selectively identify female fetuses in a society that has traditionally preferred sons over daughters. Several commentators discussed the historical, regional, and cultural roots of son preference and daughter neglect (Jeffery et al. 1984; Miller 1985; Ramanamma and Bambawale 1980) and made dire predictions of the social and demographic consequences of female-selective abortion (Dube 1983; Kumar 1983; Sudha and Rajan 1999). A group of activists known as the "Forum Against Sex Determination and Sex Pre-selection Techniques" in collaboration with several women's activists groups launched nationwide media campaigns against the "misuse" of ultrasonography and amniocentesis by married couples driven by a "mania for sons" (Ramanamma and Bambawale 1980). The campaign described the practice of female-selective abortion as one of the more recent manifestations of a traditional preference for sons in India's patriarchal social system. Numerous journalistic accounts and independent investigative reports published in popular magazines and newspapers also drew public attention to the extensive "misuse" of ultrasonography and the practice of female-selective abortion (Patel 2003; 2007).

Noteworthy among these reports is an editorial written in the *Times of India* estimating that, between 1978 and 1982, approximately 78,000 fetuses identified as female by the use the prenatal diagnostic technologies were aborted (Times of India 1982). This newspaper report, for the first time, revealed the enormity of the problem associated with prenatal sex identification and female-selective abortion in India. Researchers speculated about how the practice of female-selective abortion, if unchecked, might lead to an unbalanced sex ratio with more men than women in India's population (Jeffery et al. 1984; Miller 1985). The activists focused their efforts on advocating that the government control the availability and misuse of ultrasonography as a means to curb the growing problem of female-selective abortion (Patel 2007).

In response to intense lobbying of government officials and policy makers by women's activists groups and advocacy organizations, the Indian government proposed and implemented the Prenatal Diagnostic Techniques (Regulation and Prevention of Misuse) Act in 1996. The Prenatal Diagnostic Techniques Act bans the use of new reproductive technologies, including ultrasonography, for prenatal sex determination and deems illegal the practice of female-selective abortion. Although symbolic of a significant effort by the Indian government to deal with the consequences of prenatal sex determination technologies, scholars have described the Prenatal Diagnostic Techniques Act as an unenforceable and ineffective law (Kishwar 1995; Rutherford and Roy 2003). As demonstrated in Shahargaon, the use of ultrasonography for prenatal sex identification and the practice of female-selective abortion continued without interruption after the passage of this Act.

In this chapter, I examine the complexities of legal issues surrounding the availability and use of ultrasonography and the practice of female-selective abortion. I begin the discussion with an overview of the Prenatal Diagnostic Techniques Act and describe its key tenets for regulating the availability and use of the new reproductive technologies. I then examine the experiences and opinions of married Jat couples regarding the illegality of using ultrasonography for prenatal sex identification, along with the experiences and opinions of medical professionals who provide prenatal diagnostic services. I will use this information to assess reasons for the ineffectiveness of the Prenatal Diagnostic Techniques Act in preventing the use of ultrasonography for prenatal sex identification, and in curbing the practice of female-selective abortion. I also discuss how medical services providers continue to use ultrasonography for prenatal sex identification while avoiding prosecution and penalty.

THE PRENATAL DIAGNOSTIC TECHNIQUES (REGULATION AND PREVENTION OF MISUSE) ACT

The Prenatal Diagnostic Techniques Act was approved by the Indian parliament in 1994 and first implemented in 1996 to prevent the misuse of the new reproductive technologies for prenatal sex identification and to curb the practice of female-selective abortion. In keeping with recent advancements in reproductive technologies, the Indian government amended the Prenatal Diagnostic Techniques Act twice, first in 2002 and then in 2003, to also regulate the use of all prenatal sex-selection technologies. The amended version of the Act is also called the "Pre-conception and Prenatal Diagnostic Techniques (Prohibition and Regulation) Act." In addition to implementing the Act, the Indian government launched a nationwide campaign to educate health care providers, local law enforcement officers, and people seeking prenatal information about what the Act defines as the legal uses of new reproductive technologies. A description of the most recent version of the Act is available online at http://mohfw.nic.in/titlepage.htm. The key provisions are as follows:

1. The Act applies to all medical diagnostic centers, diagnostic laboratories, and genetic testing, counseling clinics, and manufacturers or distributors of

prenatal diagnostic technologies. It applies to all medical personnel who work at these laboratories, including doctors, diagnostic technicians, auxiliary medical staff, and administrators. The rules under the Act also cover the pregnant woman and her relatives, including her husband, who may want to know the sex of the fetus or who may seek female-selective abortion.

2. Before undergoing an ultrasonography examination, a pregnant woman, her husband, or the accompanying relative must declare in writing that she (or he) does not intend to find out the sex of the fetus.

3. All facilities using the new reproductive technologies must register with the local health and law enforcement authorities.

4. All private companies manufacturing or selling ultrasonography equipment must also register with the local health and law enforcement authorities. These companies must sell ultrasonography machines only to clinics or diagnostic centers registered under the Act, and they must report the names and address of the buyers to the local authorities.

5. All registered facilities must maintain a record of the number, names, and residential addresses of their clients seeking prenatal diagnostic procedures. All registered facilities must provide a monthly report to the local authorities listing all prenatal diagnostic tests conducted.

6. All prenatal diagnostic or screening facilities must prominently display a sign notifying their clients that the facility does not conduct sex determination tests and that doing so is a punishable act under the Act (Figure 7.1).

7. No prenatal diagnostic techniques, including ultrasonography, can be used for fetal sex identification. Medical services providers conducting prenatal diagnostic procedures cannot communicate to the pregnant woman or her relatives the sex of the fetus by words, gestures, or in any other manner.

8. Before conducting any prenatal diagnostic procedure or test, the medical practitioner must explain not only the possible side effects and risks involved, but also obtain written approval from the pregnant woman. Prenatal

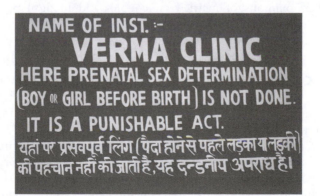

F I G U R E   7.1   Poster in Dr. Verma's clinic displaying the statement mandated by the Prenatal Diagnostic Techniques Act (© Sunil K. Khanna)

diagnostic techniques can be used only for detecting chromosomal abnormalities, genetic metabolic disorders, sex-linked genetic diseases, and birth defects. Prenatal diagnostic techniques can be used only if at least one or more of the following criteria are met:

   a. The pregnant woman is older than thirty-five years.

   b. The pregnant woman has experienced two or more miscarriages or spontaneous abortions.

   c. The pregnant woman was exposed to certain drugs, chemicals, radiation, or infections that may be harmful to the fetus.

   d. The pregnant woman has a family history of mental health problems or physical deformities.

9. Advertising of these technologies for purposes of prenatal sex selection and identification is prohibited.

10. Local health and law enforcement authorities can conduct random checks on clinics performing prenatal diagnostic tests and examine their records for inconsistencies.

11. Any person breaking any aspect of the Act must pay a penalty of up to 10,000 rupees ($240), which may extend up to 100,000 rupees ($2,400) for repeat violations.

12. Any person found guilty under the Act will serve a prison sentence for up to three years, which may extend up to five years for repeat violations (Figure 7.2).

Although the Prenatal Diagnostic Techniques Act has been recognized by some activists groups as a step in the right direction, others have expressed skepticism regarding the effectiveness of the Act in preventing the use of ultrasonography for prenatal sex identification and in deterring couples from seeking female-selective abortion (Patel 2007). Several critics have discussed the impracticality of enforcing the Act suggesting that legislation alone cannot prevent female feticide (Kishwar 1995; Sagar 2007). In the subsequent sections of this chapter, I examine the effectiveness of the Act through the experiences and opinions of married Jat couples and medical practitioners in Shahargaon.

CONSEQUENCES OF CRIMINALIZATION

During my field visits in 1993, 1995, and 1999, I noticed several outdoor billboards advertising prenatal sex determination test on the main road, in alleys inside the village, and in lanes all along the residential and commercial areas surrounding Shahargaon. Local newspapers regularly carried advertisements for diagnostic and abortion centers that provided prenatal sex determination and sex-selective abortion services (see Chapter 5). In some advertisements, diagnostic centers used son preference as justification for the cost of ultrasonography and abortion. Some advertisements even suggested that paying for these medical

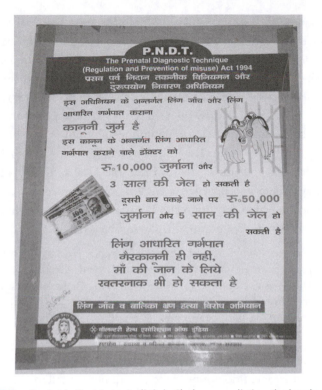

FIGURE 7.2   Poster in Dr. Verma's clinic in Shahargaon listing the legal consequences of breaking the Prenatal Diagnostic Techniques Act

SOURCE: Voluntary Health Association of India

services makes financial sense because the couples will not have to bear the cost of dowry. However, in recent years as the awareness of the Prenatal Diagnostic Techniques Act has increased, I noticed a decline in public advertisements of ultrasonography for prenatal sex identification in the urban markets surrounding Shahargaon. No medical providers I interviewed for this study display such billboards.

Married Jat couples showed only limited awareness of the Act. Although most knew that it was illegal to seek prenatal sex identification, they did not think that anyone would be arrested for doing so. Illegality meant only that they would have to pay extra to the doctor at the diagnostic clinic. Dr. Parveen Seth, the owner of the New Delhi Diagnostic Clinic located in the Shahargaon market, expressed his strong opinion:

I do not think people in this village need more advertising about the uses of ultrasonography. They know about its only use and that is to know the sex of the fetus. They have known this for the past ten years. As usual, our government has been late in responding to the call to root out the menace of female feticide. There has already been enough advertising throughout the 1990s. Frankly, people do not learn about ultra-sonography from billboards or posters. They get this information from their friends and neighbors. The Prenatal Diagnostic Techniques Act has not stopped people from demanding these services or doctors from pro-viding these services in a clandestine manner. Married couples who want sons demand it and doctors who need money fulfill this demand. In fact, doctors charge more money for ultrasonography now than they used to charge before the Prenatal Diagnostic Techniques Act. They charge more money because now they have to bribe the local officials to look the other way. There will never be a law that would prevent couples from seeking sex-selective abortion. The Prenatal Diagnostic Techniques Act is simply useless. It creates more hassles for everyone.

Several married Jat women in Shahargaon reported that banning the use of ultrasonography for prenatal sex determination and the law against female-selective abortion has not deterred anyone from using these services. Both Jat men and women confirmed Dr. Seth's assertion that the Prenatal Diagnostic Techni-ques Act has only made ultrasonography tests and female-selective abortion more expensive. According to Sohan Lal:

> I know killing daughters is a crime, whether it is before birth, after birth, or after their marriage. I do not need the government to tell me that. But the world has changed and so have people. When I was young I had not even heard the word abortion. I only heard it in my old age when ultrasound became available in the village market. Nowadays people in the village talk about it casually all the time. Like everything else that our government does, this whole talk about putting people in jail for ultrasound or abortion is just to scare people. I think government wants police to make more money by taking bribes from innocent hardworking people.

One of the consequences of the Prenatal Diagnostic Techniques Act has been that the practice of sex-selection has made bribes commonplace to keep the eyes of the law looking the other way. Sandhya, a Jat woman in her early thirties explained:

> The doctor at one of the local clinics told me that I will have to pay an extra fee of one thousand rupees [approximately $24] if I want to know the sex of the fetus. The lady doctor told me that she has to bribe the local policeman and the health inspector who visits her clinic every month. I have heard from other women that cops and inspectors collect bribes from other clinics on a regular basis. They ask for extra money from all doctors even though I know that some of the doctors do not tell the sex of the fetus. They harass those doctors who refuse to pay bribes.

Thus, the implementation of the Prenatal Diagnostic Techniques Act has led a sudden increase in the "unofficial" cost of prenatal sex determination tests. Medical practitioners complain about police harassment to justify charging higher fees. In some cases, the doctors and the police have agreed on a fixed amount of money (*hafta*) of one thousand rupees (approximately $24) as the standard bribe to be paid on a weekly or biweekly basis. The Prenatal Diagnostic Techniques Act has become a means for the local health and law enforcement authorities to harass doctors working in diagnostic centers and clinics and has not had the intended effect of preventing the use of ultrasonography for prenatal sex identification or the practice of female-selective abortion.

"QUICK AND CHEAP" PRENATAL SEX IDENTIFICATION TESTS

A billboard outside a local diagnostic clinic advertises "Quick and Cheap" tests. Dr. Prateep Bandhu who runs this clinic claims that his "Quick and Cheap" tests allow married couples to have a "child with options." When I asked him to clarify the meaning of the phrase "child with options," he smiled and said, "You know what I mean. Everyone who comes here wants a son. My tests give them the option to have a son." Dr. Bandhu has told me that he has a doctoral degree in biochemistry. He claimed that his clinic is "registered" with the local health authorities and that he has acquired a government license for providing prenatal diagnostic services through unconventional, but scientifically reliable procedures that are cheap and take less time. Despite my repeated requests, Dr. Bandhu refused to show me either his registration certificate or his practicing license. He allowed me to observe his interactions with clients only if I assured him that I would not take any pictures or use a tape recorder to record his conversations.

In conducting a routine examination, Dr. Bandhu performs a series of tests, which only take two minutes. Since Dr. Bandhu's clinic is not equipped with an appropriate machine, the tests do not involve ultrasonography. Instead, Dr. Bandhu performs a simple blood test on the pregnant woman. Before conducting the test, he meets with the woman and her husband (or the accompanying relative) in the clinic and assures them of the scientific reliability of his testing procedure. During this conversation, he collects information on the woman's pregnancy history and develops a cordial relationship with her and the accompanying relative, ensuring them that he understands their "needs and desires" and that "with the help of god they will be blessed with a son." He then proceeds to collect a blood sample from the woman by pricking her finger with a needle and asks her to wait outside in the patient lounge. Back in the laboratory, he prepares a smear slide of the blood sample, stains it, and observes it under a light microscope. Based on a set of parameters that Dr. Bandhu refused to share with me, he identified the sex of the fetus. He then communicates the results to the woman and/or her relative. In most cases he reports that the test indicates the conception of a daughter. This dramatic disclosure is immediately followed by an assurance that

Dr. Bandhu can take care of the client's "problem" by referring her to a known and reliable abortion clinic. He then receives a pre-established kickback fee from the abortion clinic. In most cases, the referral is by telephone or by a messenger. Dr. Bandhu contends that his technique is scientifically valid and that it is not illegal under the Prenatal Diagnostic Techniques Act because it does not involve the use of ultrasonography or any other diagnostic/imaging technology.

Although peculiar in terms of its testing procedures, Dr. Bandhu's clinic otherwise is not an anomaly. Many such "unregistered" diagnostic clinics, in collaboration with abortion clinics, commercialize on people's ignorance about the Prenatal Diagnostic Techniques Act, their lack of knowledge about the scientific basis for prenatal diagnostic tests, and their strong desire for sons. More importantly, such phony diagnostic procedures expose women to serious health risks. Most Jat women reported that they would never use unreliable clinics, although Sushila believed that others might do so, "Married couples desperate for a son would believe anyone who gives them any hope."

In contrast to Dr. Bandhu's "quick and cheap" prenatal sex identification test of dubious technique which is lacking scientific credibility, the *British Medical Journal* recently reported the availability of a simple but scientifically reliable blood test to reveal the sex of the fetus (Tanne 2005). The test is called the "Baby Gender Mentor Test." It can be administered as early as the fifth week of pregnancy. The test involves collecting a small blood sample by a finger prick of the pregnant woman and analyzing the sample in a laboratory for fetal DNA. The clinical applications of the test include identifying genetic disorders and diagnosing Down's syndrome. At present, the test is available only in the United States and costs approximately $250. However, it is only a matter of time when more affordable versions of the test will be available and used for prenatal sex identification in India. Regulating the availability and use of the Baby Gender Mentor Test under the Prenatal Diagnostic Techniques Act will be a difficult task. Because of the simple procedure required for sample collection, people can easily perform the Baby Gender Mentor Test in the privacy of their homes. The blood samples then go to local privately-run laboratories for sex identification. The test is affordable and can identify the sex of the fetus at an early stage in pregnancy even before the pregnancy becomes noticeable to others. Considering the lack of success of the Prenatal Diagnostic Techniques Act in regulating the availability and use of ultrasonography for prenatal sex identification, it is likely to be grossly ineffective in regulating the Baby Gender Mentor Test.

THE "COSTS AND BENEFITS" OF CRIMINALIZATION

Doctors and diagnosticians providing prenatal sex identification and abortion services practice a kind of collusion to circumvent the Prenatal Diagnostic Techniques Act. One of the commonly used strategies currently evident in the urban markets surrounding Shahargaon involves deliberately separating prenatal diagnostic centers from abortion clinics. Most diagnostic centers in Shahargaon do not provide abortion services and vice versa. Doctors running diagnostic centers receive indirect kickbacks to refer pregnant women to abortion clinics. This strategy allows for a profitable alliance between the two clinics. It also allows doctors at abortion clinics to claim that they are providing only abortion services, which are legal under the Medical Termination of Pregnancy Act.

Another commonly employed strategy involves using portable ultrasonography machines to perform off-site prenatal sex determination tests. Doctors perform these tests at satellite clinics located in rural areas or even in the homes of their clients. All diagnostic centers located in markets surrounding Shahargaon and in the nearby town of Mandi have portable ultrasonography units to use for regular house-calls. Doctors at two diagnostic centers in Shahargaon have jointly purchased a refurbished portable ultrasonography machine (Model Logiq 100 by General Electric) for $10,000. They described the machine as a "sound business strategy" to take advantage of a growing need for providing diagnostic services in the homes of their clients.

These changes collectively represent the emergence of a privately funded sex-selection industry. The industry has recognized the income potential in marketing new reproductive technologies. By conservative estimates, the sex-selection industry in India is a multi-million dollar business (Baldauf 2006). General Electric Company (GE) in collaboration with WIPRO, an India-based company, is the largest supplier of ultrasonography equipment in India. Other major suppliers of ultrasonography equipment include Toshiba Corporation, Siemens AG, and Phillips Electronics. According to a recent report published in *The Wall Street Journal*, ultrasound sales in India reached up to $77 million in 2006. These figures mark a 10% increase from the sales in 2005 (Wonacott 2007). Most clinics are equipped with at least two ultrasonography machines manufactured by General Electric. The cost of a new ultrasonography machine ranges between $8,000 and $15,000 depending upon the model. Presuming that on average a doctor conducts five to eight ultrasonography tests per day and earns a profit of about $20 per test, a clinic can pay back the cost of the machine in less than six months. Therefore, doctors consider the cost of the machine as a small investment compared to the anticipated profits from a high demand for prenatal testing. Although clinics are required by law to register under the Prenatal Diagnostic Techniques Act, several doctors consider the registration process to be too cumbersome and time consuming. In some cases they bribe the local health officials and/or police to avoid incurring penalties for not registering. Some clinics underreport the number of machines they have or completely fail to disclose the purchase of mobile ultrasonography equipment. According to Dr. Bhandari, a radiologist working at a diagnostic clinic in Mandi:

> Everyday we get salesmen from ultrasound companies asking us to buy new machines, portable machines, or even second-hand [refurbished] ultrasound machines. First they make us sign some paperwork to assure them that we will not use the machine for prenatal sex identification. Then they tell us how to get around the Prenatal Diagnostic Techniques Act. They tell us that we are not required to register if we buy a second-hand

[refurbished] machine or a mobile ultrasonography machine. I am not sure
if that is correct; but I do not have the time to cross-check this information.
I have a practice to run; so I simply believe what the salesman tells me.

Clearly, the sex-selection industry has been successful in pursuing an array of
profitable business strategies because of the absence of an effective system regulating the availability and use of new reproductive technologies, an increasing
demand for ultrasonography and other prenatal sex identification technologies,
and people's limited understanding of the Prenatal Diagnostic Techniques Act. In
an attempt to strictly regulate the use of ultrasonography for prenatal sex determination without effectively addressing the grassroots realities of its availability
and widespread use, government policies have contributed to an increase of
malpractice in performing prenatal diagnostic and abortion procedures.

SEX-SELECTIVE CONCEPTION

Sex-selective conception or sex-preselection is an emerging trend in urban India,
especially in selectively conceiving a male fetus. The procedure involves a
combination of Ericsson's sperm separation technique and ultrasonography.
Dr. Ronald Ericsson, a reproductive physiologist in the United States, visited India
in 1986 to promote his technique, which allows the separation of X-carrying
sperm from Y-carrying sperm. The Y-chromosome contains 3.5% less DNA than
an X-chromosome and can be distinguishably stained by quinacrine (Holmes and
Hoskins 1987). Once the sperm have been separated by using differential cen-
trifugation or flow cytometry, the woman undergoes an ultrasonography exam to
pinpoint the exact time of her ovulation. Theoretically speaking, injecting the
woman with Y-carrying sperm guarantees the conception of a male fetus. Although expensive, pre-conceptional sex-selection procedure is available in New
Delhi at clinics providing in-vitro fertilization (IVF) or pre-implantation genetic
diagnosis (PGD) services. These clinics offer choices of sex-selection procedures to
couples who want to have children of a certain sex. Most Jat married couples are
unaware of such pre-conceptional or pre-implantation sex-selection procedures.
The few couples who know have only limited knowledge. However, they are
unwilling to use these procedures because of the high cost and time involved.
According to Ramdhan, a 25-year-old Jat man:

> A clinic in central Delhi guarantees that a married couple can have a son.
> My friend knows a doctor who works at the clinic. He told me that this
> doctor can make sure that the woman gets pregnant with a boy. He also
> told me that it costs a lot of money and takes many days. But they
> guarantee that the child will be a boy. I told my wife about it, but we
> think that we do not have that much money. So we will just use the
> ultrasound machine to know the sex of the fetus. Hopefully, we will be
> lucky and will not have to go for an abortion.

Like Ramdhan, all other couples in Shahargaon expressed a preference for the combined use of ultrasonography and sex-selective abortion over that of sex-selective conception.

In the last two decades, the sex-selection industry has introduced other questionable methods and techniques mimicking the promises of the pre-conceptional procedures. Promoters of this lucrative business have introduced special diets, coital techniques and positions, and drugs promising "selective conception of sons", claiming that they give married couples the power to choose the sex of their children. One of the most popular drugs promising sex-selective conception carries the trade name SELECT. According to the manufacturer, Gujarat-based Vasu Pharmaceuticals, the drug guarantees the conception of a boy. The manufacturer guarantees that if a pregnant woman takes the drug as prescribed, i.e. forty-five days after her last menstrual period, she would conceive a male fetus (Unnikrishnan 1993). The promotional literature for SELECT claims that the drug is a panacea for India's social and population problems as it will support family planning, discourage the dowry system and the birth of unwanted daughters, reduce discrimination against women, and fulfill the lasting desire of a couple to have a son. Although the sale of the drug would be considered illegal under the Prenatal Diagnostic Techniques Act, several other drugs and potions, claiming similar benefits, are widely available. A recent study on the use of sex-selection drugs by pregnant women in north India suggests that such drugs are either sold by local practitioners or are available for purchase in grocery stores and pharmacies (Bandyopadhyay and Singh 2007). The study also reports the two drugs contained progesterone and testosterone, and tested positive for natural steroids.

Practitioners of indigenous medicine in Shahargaon claim that several ancient texts in Ayurveda—the Indian traditional medical system—describe herbs, timings and positions for intercourse, and dietary restrictions that practitioners can recommend for the conception of a son or for changing the sex of the fetus from female to male. They see an increasing demand for their services in the emerging sex-selection industry. They openly sell their indigenously-made, natural, but reliable potions, herbs, drugs, and techniques ensuring the conception of a son. They promote the products by invoking religious metaphors and the power of traditional medicine. However, only a few Jat couples reported using Ayurvedic drugs or following dietary recommendations by indigenous practitioners to conceive a son. Most couples dismissed the claims of sex-selective conception as unreliable or simply as efforts made by the local practitioners to make money. Although unpopular in Shahargaon, the introduction of SELECT in the Indian market and the active promotion of other similar drugs and potions for sex-selection by practitioners of traditional medicine demonstrate an attempt by the local entrepreneurs in the sex-selection industry to promote an indigenous version of the western sex-selection technology similarly capitalizing on the traditional preference for sons. Although sex-selective conception is deemed illegal under the Prenatal Diagnostic Techniques Act, it is extremely difficult to prevent the sale of the indigenous sex-selection drugs, techniques, and diets for the same reasons that make it difficult to regulate the use of ultrasonography for prenatal sex identification and female-selective abortion.

LIMITATIONS OF THE LAW AND FUTURE PROSPECTS

As a legal tool, the Prenatal Diagnostic Techniques Act is fraught with problems associated with identifying those who are most likely to break the law and then catching them in the act. Most importantly, the Prenatal Diagnostic Techniques Act does not constitute a policy aimed at improving the social status of daughters and reducing preference for sons. In Shahargaon, the Prenatal Diagnostic Techniques Act does not discourage Jat couples from using ultrasonography for prenatal sex identification as a private, affordable, and effective means of realizing son preference. Nor does the Act serve as an effective deterrent against the "illegal" use of ultrasonography by members of the medical community who are driven primarily by the economic interests. According to Madhu Kishwar, the editor of *Manushi: A Journal about Women and Society*:

> It is time that we face the fact that the laws that have been enacted to prohibit prenatal sex determination will not work given and political and administrative level of function in our country. The more stringent law attempting to prohibit consensual behavior, the greater the likelihood that it will be used primarily for making money by officials. The police know the location and activity of sex determination clinics; they collect regular bribes from the doctors as protection money, just as they do from brothel owners in states where prostitution is banned (Kishwar 1995: 17).

The local law enforcement officials and health agency representatives, who are supposed to be day-to-day enforcers of the Prenatal Diagnostic Techniques Act, often serve as enablers of the use of ultrasonography for prenatal sex identification. They collect bribes from clinics that conduct prenatal sex-selection tests and those that provide sex-selective abortions. This profitable nexus between the clinics and the law enforcement personnel is quite widespread in Shahargaon and Mandi. The cost of bribing the police ultimately falls on those who use the illegal services. Jat couples report paying additional fees of up to 500 rupees (approximately $12) to clinicians for providing prenatal sex identification or female-selective abortion services in a clandestine manner. The result is a system of corruption that involves couples seeking prenatal knowledge, doctors communicating that knowledge, and law enforcement authorities receiving kickback fees for ignoring these illegal transactions.

Based on my long-term ethnographic research in Shahargaon and interviews with doctors providing diagnostic and abortion services, I have learned that the Prenatal Diagnostic Techniques Act is ineffective for several reasons.

1. Documenting the act in which the medical provider or auxiliary staff working at the clinic communicates information pertaining to prenatal sex identification is extremely difficult, if not impossible. Such communication occurs in private between medical professionals whose inclination is to assist their

clients and families prepared to ignore legal prohibitions to realize their preference for sons.

2. The Act contains no mechanism to hold any individual persons legally liable for aiding or facilitating prenatal sex determination tests. In addition to the woman herself, facilitators include members of her immediate family and her broader social network who provide information about clinics that perform prenatal sex determination tests.

3. Regulating the sale and distribution of ultrasonography machines and other equipment used for prenatal sex identification, as opposed to a variety of legitimate purposes, is extremely difficult.

4. Clinicians do not record every case of prenatal testing, especially when the testing involves portable ultrasound machines in clients' homes or at an off-site facility.

5. Most government agencies lack appropriate training and resources to ensure effective and corruption-free coordination among law enforcement groups, local and regional health authorities, and the various administrative agencies involved in monitoring and enforcing the Act.

A legislative and regulatory approach is not sufficient. The Prenatal Diagnostic Techniques Act is removed from the cultural realities that drive the demand for new reproductive technologies. The Act criminalizes behavior that cannot be controlled, and does not serve as a mechanism to change the behavior of those seeking and providing prenatal diagnostic and abortion services. According to Sagar (2007: 198):

> ...while it [Prenatal Diagnostic Techniques Act] is necessary, ultimately legislation is not sufficient to prevent female elimination. Nor can it be a substitute for cultural changes and consciousness-raising at a countrywide level. Efforts to tackle this problem cannot be fragmented but need to be comprehensive. Not only do we have to tackle and control our technology, we need to improve the social position of women. There can, therefore, never be a simple approach to tackling this problem. The issue of female elimination cannot be witnessed in isolation from the social, cultural, and economic context of people's lives.

If the goal is to prevent the "misuse" of ultrasonography and stop the practice of female-selective abortion, then the issue of female feticide must also be recognized and defined as a social problem, not exclusively as a legal problem. Without fear of legal reprisal, Jat couples in Shahargaon are using ultrasonography for prenatal sex identification and female selective abortion as means to build their families of desired size and sex composition. Understanding the vividly intricate and intersecting views of Jat couples on son preference, gender status and roles in Shahargaon, and the choices available for regulating family size and sex composition, are crucial to developing new strategies to prevent prenatal sex-selection at present, and pre-conceptual sex selection in the future.

Chapter 8

✳

Advocating for Change

On July 21, 2007, voters in India elected Pratibha Patil as the first woman president in sixty years since the country became independent from Great Britain. Observers in India and across the world hailed the election as a landmark step toward women's rights and achieving gender equality across the entire country. From 1966 to 1977, Indira Gandhi served as India's first woman prime minister, the most powerful political office in India's parliamentary system. Although important, such political gains and the attention drawn to them primarily reflect the achievements of urban middle-to-upper class educated women. The election of a woman president or prime minister has had only marginal impact on the lives of the rural, poor, uneducated women. In the past two decades, India has emerged as a new economic power on the world stage, and is beginning to deliver on its promises of economic growth. People living in mega cities and urbanizing towns are experiencing improvements in economic status, easy access to technology, improved health care facilities, and increasing opportunities for education and employment. However, these positive changes belie increasing economic and health status disparities, uneven infrastructural development, and gender inequality that define everyday life in much of the country.

The recently retired Chief Justice of India, Y. K. Sabharwal, eloquently describes the above contradictions in contemporary Indian society:

Everyone says that we have come a long way since our independence more than half a century ago. Indeed, we have made significant scientific and technological progress and we churn out some of the brightest minds every year in every area possible. But when I hear of female infanticide and female feticide let alone the gender discrimination everywhere else or when I see the statistics showing the skewed sex ratio, it makes me think that all this progress is absolutely worthless. On many occasions I reflect on the progress that women have made in our country and I feel proud—we had our first female head of state decades ago and women in politics, sports, literature and other arts continue to perform outstandingly. Yet, this pride is short lived and it dissipates into a kind of horror and despair with the knowledge that despite such demonstrations of brilliance by Indian women, our society fails to even secure them existence (Y. K. Sabharwal 2006: 2).

Justice Sabharwal's comments point to the great paradox of social life where improvement in income, education, and health, technological innovation, and participation in the global economy have not predictably resulted in opportunities and improvement for all. Recent studies suggest an alarmingly high level of gender disparity in terms of health and education outcomes. In her book, *India: Globalization and Change*, the author Pamela Shurmer-Smith remarks:

> …globalization is accompanied by a thinning of internal solidarity. Elite Indians have increasing amounts in common (economically, politically, and culturally) with English speakers elsewhere in the world…For the poor, the outcomes of globalization are not qualitative lifestyle changes and westernized consumer goods, but more of what went before: more rural indebtedness, more landlessness, more food shortages, more child labor, more casualization of work, more violence and intimidation (Shurmer-Smith 2000: 2).

Improvements in India's economy and infrastructure have ushered the country and its people into a new era of global connectivity with improved access to technology and information. These recent developments, coupled with the success of India's population policies and programs, have resulted in a slow but steady decline in the country's population growth rate. However, these changes have not led to an erosion of son preference. In fact, there is evidence to suggest that it has increased as a consequence of an awkward "interaction" between historically specific and culturally constructed behavior and recent socioeconomic changes (Croll 2000; Khanna 1997). Despite embracing the larger global community through the media, economic opportunities, and infrastructural development, India's cultural traditions strongly influence decision-making processes regarding family size and sex composition, allocation of household resources, and participation in income generating activities by men and women.

In comparison to girls, boys are more likely to receive a favorable allocation of household resources resulting in better nutritional status, enhanced educational and employment opportunities, and more decision-making power. With the increased availability of new reproductive technologies, discrimination against girls can now occur before they are born. As my Shahargaon research shows, son preference is the key reason for discrimination against girls during the prenatal period. Prenatal discrimination against girls is a two-step process involving the use of ultrasonography for prenatal sex identification and the selective abortion of female fetuses. Prenatal sex selection is an outcome of an awkward, perhaps even ironic, convergence of community-specific characteristics promoting a strong preference for sons, government family planning policies advocating for a small family size, and the larger market-driven forces that facilitate easy access to the new reproductive technologies, including ultrasonography.

PATRIARCHY AND NEW REPRODUCTIVE TECHNOLOGIES IN ASIA

Holism—examining human behavior and condition from all aspects of history and culture, and cross-cultural comparison—looking for similarities and differences in human behavior and condition across cultures—constitute two of the important building blocks of anthropological inquiry. A comparative perspective increases understanding of the reasons for son preference across societies, similarities and differences in availability and use of new reproductive technologies, and to place what we learn in particular cultural situations into a larger global context.

Since the 1960s new reproductive technologies, especially prenatal diagnostic technologies, have been routinely used in health care worldwide (see Chapter 5). Given that son preference is a cross-cultural characteristic shared by many communities in other parts of the world, we can infer the widespread use of ultrasonography for identifying female fetuses leading to female-selective abortion. Numerous studies support this inference, with the most compelling examples existing in China and South Korea (Bossen 2007; Croll 2000; Lavely et al. 2001; Shuzhuo et al. 2007). The sex ratios at birth and in the child population in both countries show an excess of males over females, suggesting that married couples motivated by a strong preference for sons are using new reproductive technologies to select against girls (Kim 2004). However, a recent study based on an analysis of the Korean National Fertility and Family Health Surveys in 1991 and 2003 reports a trend of balancing of sex ratio in the country, especially after the mid-1990s (Chung and Das Gupta 2007). The researchers suggest the observed trend can be attributed to a combined effect of increase in women's education and employment levels, improved family income and living standards, urbanization, and gradual changes in social norms leading to a decline in son preference. Although other countries in Asia can learn from the above-mentioned example, compared to India and China, South Korea is a small country with a relatively homogenous population. In the last two decades, it has experienced unprecedented and nationwide industrial and infrastructural development. In contrast, the trend of development and industrialization in India and China can be at best described as uneven.

In the following section, I summarize the information available on sex ratio distribution in China in order to make a case that Chinese couples are using new reproductive technologies for prenatal sex identification and are practicing female-selective abortion.

"MISSING" GIRLS IN CHINA

China has been the most populated country in the world for quite some time. Based on current estimates, China's total population presently is more than 1.3 billion and is expected to grow by another 100 million by 2050 (Riley 2004). Detailed analyses of national and regional survey data show that the current overall sex ratio in China is 936 females per 1000 males, and that the sex ratio becomes sharply masculine in the child population. Researchers have estimated China's total child sex ratio to be 855 girls per 1000 boys (Chu 2003; Das Gupta et al. 2003). Ding and Kesketh (2006) report an average sex ratio of 870 females per 1000 males in a large sample of rural and urban women (39,585 women and 73,202 pregnancies) surveyed by the Chinese National Family Planning Commission. Some provinces in China have reported even more radically skewed child sex ratios favoring boys. In a recent study of the 2000 population census figures from China, a group of researchers report that the sex ratio at birth was abnormally low (<800 females per 1000 males) in the provinces of Shanxi, Henan, Anhui, Zhejiang, Jiangxi, Fujian, and Guangdong (Shuzhuo et al. 2007).

The similarity between India and China is clear:

> ...the deterioration of child sex ratio has run parallel in China and India over three decades...in both countries, fertility decline has been accompanied...by a strong desire by couples to intervene on the sex composition of their offspring...sex-selective abortions are probably the main cause today for the rapid degradation of child sex ratio [in China] (Guilmoto and Attane 2007: 109).

Traditional preference for sons in Chinese society and strict enforcement of the country's one-child policy, at least in urban areas, have synergistically influenced married couples' decisions to manipulate the sex composition of their families by using ultrasonography and female-selective abortion (Banister 2004; Ding and Hesketh 2006). In her study of the shortage of girls in China, Banister (2004) claims that the "missing girls" in China's population can be largely attributed to the use of sex-selection technology. She asserts:

> ...after ultrasound became widely available, the shortage of girls emerged in many provinces where it had not been visible before. In provinces where son preference had already been evident, the new technology added sex-selective abortion to the existing ways to dispose of unwanted daughters...the combination of continuing son preference, low fertility and technology is causing the shortage of girls in China and other parts of Asia (Banister 2004: 38–39).

Other researchers point out that parental bias favoring sons has resulted in higher mortality rates of girls in comparison to boys, which in turn has contributed to masculine sex ratios in the country's child population (Arnold et al. 1998, 2000; Burgess and Zhuang 2000). As in the case of India, premature deaths of girl children may have an effect on sex ratios but not the dominant effect. Clearly, India and China exhibit similar patterns of sex ratio distribution, son preference, with similar historical and cultural underpinnings resulting in a convergence of demographic consequences in terms of regional and national sex ratios favoring men.

COMPARING INDIA AND CHINA

In a classic study using cross-cultural data, Williamson (1976) ranked parental preference for sons or daughters across many societies. She observed a "strong" or "very strong" preference for sons among married couples in India and China. Ethnographic evidence from both countries suggests that parental preference for sons most commonly results in a biased allocation of household resources, especially spending on food and health care that favors sons and reduces the survivability of daughters. Proverbs and folk songs in both countries reinforce the social and economic benefits of a son and label a daughter as a liability. The Chinese proverb "more sons, more happiness" (*duozi duofu*) is popular in many Chinese communities, suggesting a strong preference for sons (Yan 2003). Chinese couples, especially in peasant communities, believe that the birth of a son brings joy and happiness and must be celebrated by the family and community (Croll 2000).

In spite of regional variability, family systems in India and China are characterized by a patrilineal social system[1] (Das Gupta et al. 2003). The key reasons for a strong parental preference for sons include characteristics commonly associated with patrilineal systems—girls being considered unproductive members of the family, economic liabilities, and temporary residents in their parents' homes before marriage.

> As long as the custom persists for women and their future productivity to be totally absorbed by their in-laws, parents are likely to perceive daughters as a drain and prefer to raise sons. Women can contribute little to their parents' welfare, so even when levels of women's education and formal sector labor force participation increase, the fruits of these go to her husband's home. Even though women can gain considerable power in the household in their old age, this depends on having sons who support their mother's voice in the household at the expense of their own wives. In short, the vulnerability of women in these settings is well-designed for reinforcing and perpetuating itself with little need for direct reinforcement from the male world (Das Gupta et al. 2003: 28–29).

Son preference, excess female mortality, and masculine sex ratios are some of the most enduring cultural and demographic characteristics of communities in India and China. Sex ratios indicating a surplus of men and a corresponding deficit of women in India and China are demographic trends that have global, as well as local and regional consequences (Isabelle 2006; Sen 2003). According to the most recent population estimates, India and China together account for more than 40% of the world population and are recording only a modest decline in their population growth rate (Fan and Gulati 2008). Both countries have long recognized the problems associated with their population size and the need to control population

---

1. A typical patrilineal system is male-focused. A woman marries outside her own patrilineage and her children belong to the husband's lineage. Family name and property are inherited in the male line and family resources are controlled by men.

growth. Considering the regional variation in economic status and the rate of population growth, China implemented a population policy that allows married couples living in urban areas to have only one child (One Child Policy) and limits those living in rural areas to two children per family (Attane 2002). China's population control policy employs local birth control workers in villages, work places, and neighborhoods and relies on strong state intervention in enforcement to the extent that some observers have described it as a "coercive birth limitation policy" (Guilmoto and Attane 2007: 112). In contrast, India adopted a series of population control programs culminating in a National Population Policy that promoted the benefits of small family size and encouraged the voluntary participation of its people.[2]

After nearly three decades of policy implementation, both countries have reported a sustained decline in fertility rates and record economic growth. However, their populations continue to show a significant decline in the number of women compared to men. In particular, sex ratios at birth in India and China are starkly masculine, suggesting a significant deviation from the natural sex ratio at birth[3] (Banister 2004; Croll 2000). The increasingly masculine sex ratio at birth, at least in part, is related to selective abortion of female fetuses identified by the use of ultrasonography (Ding and Hesketh 2006). Although the use of ultrasonography for prenatal sex identification and the practice of female-selective abortion are illegal in both countries, community-level studies show that in practice married couples use these services to avoid the birth of an unwanted daughter (Oomman and Ganatra 2002). In a review of the effect of China's One-Child Policy, Hesketh et al. (2005) point out that the implementation of the one-child policy in 1979 marked the beginning of a well-documented decrease in the number of women in China's population, and that this decrease has been most severe in the child population. This observation is supported by a study on abortion patterns and sex ratio at birth in rural Yunnan showing that in spite of legal prohibition against sex-selective abortion, couples required to limit the size of their families realize their preference for sons by strategically using prenatal sex determination tests and female-selective abortions to avoid the birth of an unwanted daughter (Lofstedt et al. 2004).

Although the use of ultrasonography for prenatal sex identification and the female-selective abortion is illegal in India and China, the laws banning such practices have had little effect. Systematic ethnographic studies of this issue are scarce in both countries, but more so in China. Although India and China have different political systems and have used different population control policies, they share patrilineal cultural characteristics and a strong preference for sons by parents which constitutes the core reason for selective abortion of female fetuses. Even as the two countries experience increasing rates of urbanization, infrastructural development, and economic improvements, they are experiencing a similar

---

2. See Chapter 4 for a detailed discussion on India's National Population Policy.

3. Sex ratio at birth is also called the "primary sex ratio." It averages around 952 females per 1000 males with some variation among population across the world (Agnihotri 2000).

demographic trend in terms of "missing women" (Sen 2003) or "missing girls" (Banister 2004). To stop and reverse this trend, both countries need effective policies and sustainable programs informed by a comprehensive understanding of the emergent family-building processes and trends (see below). The population policies in both countries should be aimed not only at reducing the rate of population growth, but also at restoring balance in sex ratios.

THE PERSISTENCE OF PATRIARCHY

In this book, I have addressed an important and immensely sensitive topic by using long-term ethnographic research methods. I found that an increase in urban contact and shifts in the economic status of Shahargaon Jat families have led to an intensification of son preference. The consequences of these changes include an increased use of ultrasonography for prenatal sex identification and the practice of female-selective abortion. These changes reflect a strongly perceived need by married couples to limit their family size and reduce the number of daughters per family. I also found that the reproductive choices of married Jat couples are strongly influenced by their community's history, their sense of identity, and the cultural characteristics that define sons as assets and daughters as liabilities. The historical forces that define the Jat identity in Shahargaon as a rural peasant community strongly influence son preference in the village. The Jat community's increased exposure to the urban world of New Delhi and new economic opportunities have led to rapid shifts in subsistence patterns, the availability and consumption of resources, preferences in family size, and a reorientation in the community's relationship with its past. In keeping with the community's peasant ethos, married couples view sons as economic and political assets, adding to the strength and prestige of the family. Despite improvements in economic status, Shahargaon Jats consider daughters to be economic burdens and raising daughters in urbanizing village to be a cause for anxiety. They perceive the city of New Delhi as "corrupt and dangerous" for their "vulnerable" daughters and prefer to raise them away from the negative influences of the urban world. This often means that Jat families impose strict restrictions on the mobility of girls, limit their education and employment opportunities, and marry them off at an early age.

The Shahargaon community is in the process of redefining its peasant lifestyle and ethos in a new urban environment which offers opportunity for education, employment, and prosperity; demands changes in family type and size; and expects new rules of interaction and doing business. However, the same environment presents perceived threats to the village women and to the peasant identity of the community. At their cultural core Jat men have not fully adapted to the urban lifestyle and are not the new urbanites they claim to be. They continue to think like peasants. In their new urban world, the Jats' cultural traditions and practices constitute a persistent and enduring force. The community shares and uses their past as a lens through which they interpret the urban world and define their preferred family style of life. They see increasing contact with New Delhi as an opportunity for economic prosperity and as a formidable force acting against retaining their peasant identity. As a result the community feels threatened by individualism; its people strive to maintain their collective existence; and they regard patriarchy as their strongest cohesive force.

DIFFUSION AND REGULATION OF NEW REPRODUCTIVE TECHNOLOGY

The inventors and promoters of new reproductive technologies ignored the social impact of intrusion into the human reproductive processes. In the Indian context, the availability of the new reproductive technologies exemplifies a case of "problematic diffusion" (Luthra 1994). The notion of "problematic diffusion" proposes that, regardless of prescriptive or intended medical use of these technologies, their use will spread because married couples regard them as affordable, reliable, and a private means of avoiding the birth of an unwanted daughter and realizing son preference. Such a selective use of ultrasonography for prenatal sex identification and the practice of female-selective abortion symbolize a simultaneous embracing of "modern" medical technology to realize a "traditional" preference for sons.

Supporters of the Prenatal Diagnostic Techniques Act believed that criminalizing the acts of prenatal sex determination and sex-selective abortion would be effective in stopping these practices and paid little attention to potential flaws in the implementation of the Act under India's existing administrative and law enforcement systems. In Shahargaon I found several problems obstructing the effective implementation of this law. First, it is virtually impossible to legally monitor and regulate the private communication between medical providers and couples seeking prenatal knowledge. Second, it is impossible to hold any individual family member liable. Third, it is extremely difficult to regulate the sale and distribution of all ultrasonography machines and other equipment that may or may not be used for prenatal sex identification. Fourth, no reliable means exists to record every case of prenatal testing, especially when the testing is carried out by portable ultrasound machines in clients' homes or another off-site facility. Finally, key enforcing stakeholders—health officials and the police—do not have the means to control corruption and carry out effective enforcement.

In its current form, the Prenatal Diagnostic Techniques Act is removed from the cultural realities that drive the demand for new reproductive technologies. Legislative and legal means to attack the problem are not enough. Now realizing that the implementation of the Act has been ineffective, the Indian government has established a high-level regulatory committee to conduct random inspections of ultrasound clinics and other diagnostic centers to monitor the use of new reproductive technologies (Times of India 2008). Whether these inspections can be effective is questionable for the same reasons stated in the previous paragraph. Regulation and random monitoring of the availability and use of new reproductive technologies in practice amount to only symbolic steps; the key to successful implementation of the Act is making community-level changes aimed at improving the educational status of girls, encouraging women's participation in income-generation activities, and implementing a gender-conscious approach to programs and policies aimed at facilitating socioeconomic change in communities experiencing increased urban contact.

MORALITY VERSUS WOMEN'S HEALTH

The advocacy of activists and women's organizations for ending all forms of discrimination against women highlights the problematic relationship between technology and culture, and evokes a deep emotional response. Although correct in arguing that moral justification for female-selective abortion is not possible, they tend to ignore the particular concerns of married couples that override abstract notions of morality. Incentives provided by new reproductive technologies allow Indian couples to build families of desired size and composition. Moral arguments will fall on "deaf ears" without a careful and realistic understanding of why couples use ultrasonography and female-selective abortion.

Researchers have documented the negative effects of repeated abortion on women's reproductive and overall health status (Dharmraj 1995; India Council of Medical Research 1989; Pachauri 1994; 1997; 1998). Repeated female-selective abortion expose women to infections and reproductive complications seriously jeopardizing overall women's health and survival, especially in India where health researchers have long noted the absence of adequate health care services, especially those related to women's health (Rao 2004). In this context reproductive health complications are even more problematic. Advocacy efforts should include health as an important issue in community opinion-building and mobilization efforts aimed at preventing the use of ultrasonography for sex identification and the practice of female-selective abortion.

CURRENT GOVERNMENT PROGRAMS

Since the mid-1990s, the Indian government has implemented a series of programs and policy initiatives to streamline its various activities aimed at improving survival, health, and opportunities for girls. The Ministry of Women and Child Development has integrated all regional programs under an umbrella scheme called the Integrated Child Development Services Scheme (ICDS). In this context, policies and programs specifically aimed at preventing female feticide are incorporated into larger national-level programs aimed at improving the health status and survival chances of girls. These programs show a commitment by the Indian government to provide competent health care and education for girls, thus improving their chances of survival (Ministry of Women and Child Development 2007). Two of the most recently implemented programs are as follows:

1. Loved-Daughter (*Ladli*): The Loved-Daughter program, first implemented in 2005 in the state of Haryana and then in 2008 in the city of New Delhi, is aimed at reducing the incidence of female feticide, improving the sex ratio at

birth, and enhancing the survival chances of girls by providing financial incentives of up to 5000 rupees (approximately $120) per year for up to five years for the birth and survival of a second girl. This program takes into account that married couples will likely seek female-selective abortion to avoid the birth of a second daughter. Now the program in New Delhi provides enhanced benefits of up to 10,000 rupees (approximately $240) to parents for the birth and survival of a second girl.

2. Cradle-Baby (*Palna*): First implemented in 1992 in the state of Tamil Nadu, the Cradle-Baby program encourages parents to anonymously donate their unwanted daughters at state-run shelters managed by the Indian government. In 2006, the Indian government adopted this national-level program to prevent female feticide and female infanticide. The government soon will open designated cradle reception centers throughout the country to receive "unwanted" girls, who then will be sent to government-managed orphanages. The government hopes that this initiative will reduce discrimination against girls, curb the practices of female feticide and female infanticide, and restore the sex balance in India's population.

Although government reports and official state documents boast about the amount of money allocated for these two programs and the number of families receiving benefits, little information is available on program effectiveness in either case. My findings in Shahargaon suggest that both programs will have limited influence, if any, on reducing female feticide. First, married couples' decisions to avoid the birth of a second daughter are not entirely based on economic factors. Instead they reflect an ongoing adaptation to rapid urbanization, a shift in subsistence pattern, and a crisis of identity, all occurring in the context of historically grounded cultural characteristics that promote sons as economic and social assets and daughters as liabilities. The Loved-Daughter program directly addresses immediate but not long-term economic concerns for parental support, and it fails to take into account the issues of cultural identity and prestige connected with having boys. The Cradle-Baby program assumes that female feticide is primarily related to difficult choices that couples must make after the birth of an unwanted girl. However, the decision to abort a female fetus occurs after conception and before birth. An Indian woman is not likely to carry her pregnancy to full term, only to drop the baby off in an anonymous cradle-center. A strong social stigma prevents parents from abandoning their children. A mother who gives away a newborn daughter, and family members who allow it, would suffer public condemnation and humiliation. Easy availability of ultrasonography and abortion services offers Jat couples an affordable and private means to terminate an unwanted pregnancy. Since the decision to use these services occurs in the privacy of the home and the medical community gives its tacit support to carrying out necessary procedures, a mother has no incentive to bear a female fetus to full term. The Cradle-Baby program does not recognize that cultural preference, exposure to and acceptance of state-sponsored family planning policies, and the availability and affordability of ultrasonography and abortion services are driving an emergent family-building trend. Despite the existence of cradle centers, Indian couples are likely to continue to limit family size and the number of girls per family by selectively identifying and aborting female fetuses.

COMMUNITY BASED STRATEGIES

The above discussion of the limitations of the policies of the Indian government in preventing female feticide does not mean that government efforts are completely without merit. While working on these issues over the last decade or so, I have come to see government's policies as valuable, rather than irrelevant, to developing a platform for moving forward. Despite practical problems in its implementation, the Prenatal Diagnostic Techniques Act still provides a legal framework for prosecuting those who engage in the "illegal" use of new reproductive technologies or abortion services. Both the Loved-Daughter and Cradle-Baby programs show that the Indian government is committed to investing resources to prevent female feticide and improving the overall status of survival chances of girls. However, neither of these strategies can be effective in isolation.

The general focus on women's issues and special emphasis on the lives and rights of girls in government policies are important steps in the right direction, but significant gaps exist in translating these policies into effective and sustainable practice. In her study of the social underpinnings and demographic consequences of daughter neglect in India and China, Croll (2000) agrees with the above assertion:

> ...[efforts] by development agencies, governments and women's movements constitutes a valuable and welcome step, but so far these agendas and campaigns do not yet provide the attention necessary to translate policy and intervention into widespread and sustained practice or add up to a comprehensive and systematic endeavor to address the needs of daughters. Moreover, many of the present policies and interventions are themselves limited in scope and less than effective (Croll 2000: 185).

The ideals of policy are removed from everyday experiences of women and families. My case study points to a disconnection between government policies and the opinions and practices of key stakeholders. For example, while the government touts the effectiveness of its policies in regulating the use of new reproductive technologies, the medical community overwhelmingly supports making new reproductive technologies widely available to extend medical benefits to more people. Although admitting that the use of ultrasonography for prenatal sex identification is common, they strongly believe that regulating the availability and use of the technology will not change the minds of couples seeking diagnostic sex identification and female feticide. They believe that strict enforcement of the Prenatal Diagnostic Techniques Act will only increase the cost of ultrasonography and abortion services, thus forcing couples to seek these services from untrained professionals working under unhygienic conditions.

As the Baby Gender Mentor Test becomes inexpensive and widely available to identify fetal sex, it may make the regulation of new reproductive technologies a moot point. It may even make it harder to enforce the law and exacerbate the problem of gender imbalance. The key to addressing the problem of female feticide is not related to a particular technology, but instead requires investing in advocacy efforts to counter the cultural ideology that devalues women in Indian society. The efforts of activists and legislators to introduce a regulatory approach have bypassed groups in a position to bring about normative change. Future efforts should refocus to directly engage with stakeholders at the community level, including married couples, members of the medical community, community leaders, and members of village councils (*Panchayat*). Members of the village council, though likely to have culturally conservative attitudes, have a greater influence over village affairs and opinion making than does the government. Change will not take place until they become participants not only in local opinion-building efforts, but also in community-level enforcement of the Prenatal Diagnostic Techniques Act.

As an anthropologist working on a sensitive and contentious issue, I held back, though at times only with partial success, expressing my own views on female selective abortion. During my visit to Shahargaon in 2005, I started engaging married couples and members of the village council on these issues, especially informing them about the reasons for daughter discrimination and female-selective abortion. My long-term relationship with Sohan Lal—a key informant in the study and the chief of the village council (*Panchayat*)—gave me an advantage in initiating a dialogue on female-selective abortion. He played an important role in facilitating my various meetings with other members of the village council, village elders, and local religious leaders. We agreed that the village faced perpetual problems, which I discussed with them while avoiding reference to any specific cases in the community. I informed them about the negative effects of repeated abortion on women's health, the social consequences of masculine sex ratios, and the primary purpose of the Prenatal Diagnostic Techniques Act.

The village council cooperated and worked with me to propose several local measures to raise awareness of the problem of female-selective abortion in the community. These measures included:

1. Seeking cooperation from doctors who run diagnostic and abortion clinics to discourage couples from seeking prenatal sex identification and female-selective abortion.

2. Collaborating with the various local government and non–government agencies to promote awareness of the rights and values of girls; foster community support for education of girls; engage in advocacy efforts against dowry, women's seclusion, and female-selective abortion on social, health, and moral grounds.

3. Directing the village midwife and village health worker to keep records of all pregnancies, births, and child deaths in the village.

4. Recognizing that some women in the community may be forced by family members to seek female-selective abortion. The village council provides support to such women and helps them in their resistance to undergoing forced abortion.

5. Coordinating with government programs, such as Loved-Daughter program, to provide ongoing financial incentives to parents for raising daughters.

Although limited to Shahargaon, these efforts mark a beginning in the direction of building community opinion and mobilizing community opposition to the practice of female-selective abortion. Lessons from the Shahargaon study can be applied to mobilizing other communities. Such efforts must avoid placing blame while informing stakeholders about the extent of the practice of female feticide in their communities and sensitizing them to the short-term as well as long-term health and demographic consequences. Realizing that it would be ineffective in terms of cost and time to conduct detailed ethnographic studies in all target communities, health workers can cite demographic information, such as strongly masculine sex ratios at birth and in the child population, as proxy indicators of the practice of female feticide in targeted communities. Researchers and community advocates can obtain such information from various government offices, such as the Office of the Registrar General of India (Census of India), and non-government organizations to propose and implement community-level intervention programs.

LINKING POLICY WITH COMMUNITIES

In Shahargaon I found considerable variation of opinion in the community regarding the use of ultrasonography for prenatal sex identification and the practice of female-selective abortion. Although son preference and desired family size among Shahargaon Jats are rooted in cultural norms and historical circumstances, not everyone in the community conforms to a single pattern of cultural prescriptions. Individuals have different preferences for family size and reasons for desiring sons over daughters. Moreover, individual preferences are subject to change stimulated both from within and from outside the community, depending upon the larger socioeconomic and policy circumstances. Changes in opinion and practice that have already occurred in Shahargaon contradict the notion that communities and their cultural traditions are historically frozen and culturally static entities. It is time for a revised perspective on son preference, daughter neglect, and family building practices. Policy makers must seek holistic explanations grounded in and relevant to the everyday circumstances of actual lived experiences of real people.

The policy-making processes should include members of the medical community, who must clarify and fully stand behind their stated position opposing the "misuse" of ultrasonography for prenatal sex identification and the practice of female-selective abortion. Professional organizations must develop specific guidelines and regulatory principles to be followed by all medical practitioners.

Government agencies must provide necessary resources and streamline the functioning of the various branches of the government involved in enforcing the Prenatal Diagnostic Techniques Act particularly on medical practitioners (not peasants) whose actions are legitimately scrutinized in the public domain. Most importantly, the Indian government must develop effective means of communicating the mandate of the Prenatal Diagnostic Techniques Act not only to members of the medical community, but also to couples seeking prenatal sex identification. While enforcing the law against female-selective abortion, the Indian government must also effectively support a woman's right to have an abortion for other purposes.

Appropriate government agencies should collaborate with non-government organizations in launching and sustaining grassroots efforts aimed at building community opinion against female feticide. In my work with MAMTA Health Institute for Mother and Child,[4] I have participated in opinion-building efforts at the community-level and promoting participatory engagement involving government agencies, private groups, and community stakeholders. The Health Institute engages in promoting participatory and sustainable community-level intervention programs aimed at reducing gender disparity in access to and utilization of health care, making the available health services youth-friendly, and educating people about prevention of HIV/AIDS. Through their efforts, Health Institute workers are trying to raise the status of women and are involved in educating community members about gender issues. As a non-government organization, the Health Institute has been effective in observing the impacts of policies and bridging the service gap between government agencies and targeted communities. Sustainable advocacy and policy efforts aimed at preventing female feticide in India require effective linkages between government and non-government agencies such as the Health Institute.

Finally, all advocacy efforts must take into account that prenatal sex identification and female feticide do not emerge in a cultural vacuum. Collectively, they constitute a social problem and demand a social fix, not a technological fix. They represent a composite outcome of long-established patriarchal traditions exhibiting a strong preference for sons over daughters, the associated practices of patrilocality and patrilineality, people's experiences of rapid social change, and of the government family planning policies advocating for small family size. The demand for sons cannot be stopped or reduced by legislative means alone. Only by combining community-level advocacy and action with legislative means can one achieve success. Although much of the information presented in this book is specific to the historical and cultural context of the Shahargaon, I hope it will lead to developing and implementing policies, community-level programs, and other efforts aimed at curbing the use of ultrasonography for prenatal sex determination and for preventing the practice of female-selective abortion.

---

4. For more information on MAMTA's ongoing research and intervention programs, visit http://www.mamta-himc.org/.

References

Agarwal, Bina 1994 *A Field of One's Own: Gender and Land Rights in South Asia.* Cambridge: Cambridge University Press.

Agnihotri, Satish B. 2000 *Sex Ratio Patterns in the Indian Population: A Fresh Exploration.* New Delhi: Sage Publications.

Arnold, Fred, Choe, M. K., and T. K. Roy 1998 "Son Preference, the Family-Building Process and Child Mortality in India." *Population Studies* 52(3): 301–315.

Arnold, Fred, Sunita Kishor, and T. K. Roy 2002 "Sex-selective Abortion in India." *Population and Development Review* 28(4): 759–785.

Arokiasamy, Perianayagam 2007 "Sex Ratio at Birth and Excess Female Child Mortality in India: Trends, Differential and Regional Patterns." In *Watering the Neighbor's Garden: The Growing Female Deficit in Asia.* Isabella Attané and Christopher Z. Guilmoto, eds. pp. 49–72. Paris: Committee for International Co-operation and National Research in Demography.

Attané, Isabella 2002 "China's Population Policy: An Overview of its Past and Future." *Studies in Family Planning* 33(1): 103–113.

Attané, Isabella 2006 "The Demographic Impact of a Female Deficit in China, 2000–2050." *Population and Development Review* 32(4): 755–770.

Attané, Isabella and Christopher Z. Guilmoto, eds. 2007. *Watering the Neighbor's Garden: The Growing Female Deficit in Asia.* Paris: Committee for International Cooperation and National Research in Demography.

Balasubrahmanyan, V. 1986 *Contraception as if Women Mattered.* Bombay: Center for Education and Documentation.

Baldauf, Scott 2006 "India's Girl Deficit Deepest among Educated." *The Christian Science Monitor* (January 13th).

Bandyopadhyay, S. and A. J. Singh 2007 "Sex Selection through Traditional Drugs in Rural North India." *Indian Journal of Community Medicine* 31(1): 7–9.

Banister, Judith 2004 "Shortage of Girls in China Today." *Journal of Population Research* 21(1):19–45.

Basu, Alaka Malwade 1992 *Culture, the Status of Women and Demographic Behavior; illustrated with the Case of India.* Oxford: Clarendon Press.

Becker, Gay 2000 *The Elusive Embryo: How Women and Men Approach New Reproductive Technologies*. Berkeley: University of California Press.

Berreman, Gerald B. 1972 *Hindus of the Himalayas: Ethnography and Change*. Berkeley: University of California Press.

Bhat, Mari P. N. and A. J. Francis Zavier 2003 "Fertility Decline and Gender Bias in Northern India." *Demography* 40(4): 637–657.

Bhat, Mari P. N. and A. J. Francis Zavier 2007 "Factors Influencing the Use of Prenatal Diagnostic Techniques and Sex Ratio at Birth in India." In *Watering the Neighbor's Garden: The Growing Female Deficit in Asia*. Isabella Attané and Christopher Z. Guilmoto, eds. pp. 131–160. Paris: Committee for International Cooperation and National Research in Demography.

Bhatnagar, Rashmi Dube, Renu Dube, and Reena Dube 2005 *Female Infanticide in India: A Feminist Cultural History*. New York: Albany State University Press.

Booth, B. E., M. Verma, and R. S. Bari 1994 "Fetal Sex Determination in Infants in Punjab, India: Correlations and Implications." *British Medical Journal* 309(6964): 1259–1261.

Bossen, Laurel 2007 "Missing Girls, Land and Population Controls in Rural China." In *Watering the Neighbor's Garden: The Growing Female Deficit in Asia*. Isabella Attané and Christopher Z. Guilmoto, eds. pp. 207–228. Paris: Committee for International Cooperation and National Research in Demography.

Bowles, Gordon T. 1977 *The People of Asia*. London: Weidenfeld and Nicolson.

Burgess, Robin and Juzhong Zhuang 2000 *Modernization and Son Preference*. STICERD – Development Economic Papers 29. London: Suntory and Toyota International Center for Economics and Related Sciences.

Census of India 2000 *Population Projection for India & States 1996–2016*. New Delhi: Office of the Registrar General India. ULR: http://www.censusindia.net/onebillion.html

Census of India 2001 *Provisional Population Totals: India, Census of India 2001, Paper 1*. New Delhi: Office of the Registrar General.

Census of India 2001 *History of Indian Census*. New Delhi: Office of the Registrar General.

Chandrashekhar, Sripati 1946 *India's Population: Fact and Policy*. New York: The John Day Company.

Chowdhry, Prem 1994 *The Veiled Women: Shifting Gender Equations in Rural Haryana 1880–1990*. New Delhi: Oxford University Press.

Chu, Junhong 2003 "Prenatal Sex Determination and Sex-Selective Abortion in Rural Central China." *Population and Development Review* 27(2): 259–281.

Chung, Woojin and Das Gupta, Monica 2007 "Why is Son Preference Declining in South Korea? The Role of Development and Public Policy, and the Implications for China and India." *Policy Research Working Paper Series 4373*. Washington, D.C.: The World Bank.

Coale, Ansley J. 1991 "Excess Female Mortality and the Balance of Sexes in the Population: An Estimated Number of Missing Females." *Population and Development Review* 17(3): 517–523.

Comaroff, Jean 2006 "On Ethnographic Engagement." *Anthropology News* 47(9): 3.

Corea, Gena, Renate Duelli Klein, Jalna Hanmer, Helen B. Holmes, Betty Hoskins, Madhu Kishwar, Janice Raymond, Robyn Rowland, and Roberta Steinbacher 1987 *Man-Made*

Women: How New Reproductive Technologies Affect Women. Bloomington: Indiana University Press.

Croll, Elisabeth 2000 *Endangered Daughters: Discrimination and Development in Asia.* London: Routledge Press.

Das Gupta, Monica 1987 "Selective Discrimination against Female Children in Rural Punjab, India." *Population and Development Review* 13(1): 77–100.

Das Gupta, Monica 2003 "Why is Son Preference so Persistent in East and South Asia? A Cross-Country Study of China, India, and the Republic of Korea." *Journal of Development Studies* 40(2): 153–187.

Datta, Nonica 2000 *Forming an Identity: A Social History of the Jats.* New Delhi: Oxford University Press.

Davis-Floyd, Robbie E. and Carolyn F. Sargent, eds. 1997 *Childbirth and Authoritative Knowledge: Cross-Cultural Perspectives.* Berkeley: University of California Press.

Dharmraj, D. 1995 "Reproductive Tract Infections: The Issues and Priorities for India." In *Proceedings of the Workshop at Voluntary Health Association of India.* Mira Shiva, Roma Solomon, and Manila Jose, eds. pp. 35–42. New Delhi: Voluntary Health Association of India.

Ding, Qu Jian and Therese Hesketh 2006 "Family size, Fertility Preferences, and Sex Ratio in China in the Era of the One Child Family Policy: Results from National Family Planning and Reproductive Health Survey." *British Medical Journal* 333: 371–373.

Dube, Leela 1983 "Misadventures in Amniocentesis." *Economic and Political Weekly* 18: 279–280.

Edwards, Jeanette, Sarah Franklin, Eric Hirsch, Frances Price, and Marilyn Strathern, eds. 1999 *Technologies of Procreationi: Kinship in the Age of Assisted Conception.* London: Routledge.

Embers, Carole R. and Melvin Ember, eds. 2004 *Encyclopedia of Medical Anthropology: Health and Illness in the World's Cultures (Volume 2: Cultures).* New York: Kluwer Academic/ Plenum Publishers.

Fadorak, Shirley A. 2007 *Anthropology Matters!* Toronto: Broadview Press.

Fan, Shenggen and Ashok Gulati 2008 "The Dragon and the Elephant: Learning from Agricultural and Rural Reforms in China and India." *Economic and Political Weekly* 43(26–27): 137–144.

Fred, Arnold, Sunita Kishor, and T. K. Roy 2002 "Sex-Selective Abortions in India." *Population and Development Review* 28(4): 759–785.

Freed, Ruth, S. and Stanley A. Freed 1979 "Shanti Nagar: The Effects of Urbanization in a Village in North India: Sickness and Health." *Anthropological Papers of the American Museum of Natural History* 55(5). New York: American Museum of Natural History.

Freed, Ruth S. and Stanley A. Freed 1993 "Ghosts: Life and Death in North India." *Anthropological Papers of the American Museum of Natural History.* Seattle: University of Washington Press.

Freed, Stanley A. and Ruth S. Freed 1969 "Urbanization and Family Types in a North Indian village." *Southwestern Journal of Anthropology* 25(4): 342–259.

Freed, Stanley A. and Ruth S. Freed 1976 "Shanti Nagar: The Effects of Urbanization in a Village in North India: Social Organization." *Anthropological Papers of the American Museum of Natural History* 53(1). New York: American Museum of Natural History.

Freed, Stanley A. and Ruth S. Freed 1978 "Shanti Nagar: The Effects of

Urbanization in a Village in North India: Aspects of Economy, Technology, and Ecology." *Anthropological Papers of the American Museum of Natural History* 55(1). New York: American Museum of Natural History.

Ghosh, Abantika 2005 "City's Tony Colonies have Worst Sex Ratio." *The Times of India* (August 3).

Gill, G. K. 1998 "Female Feticide as a Contemporary Cultural Practice in the Punjab." *Dialectical Anthropology* 23(2): 203–213.

Gillis, Anna Maria 1995 "Sex Selection and Demographics: Population Biologists use China as a Model to Theorize about Culture and Evolution." *BioScience* 45(6): 384–386.

Ginsburg, Faye D. and Rayna Rapp, eds. 1995 *Conceiving the New World Order: The Global Politics of Reproduction.* Berkeley: University of California Press.

Gittelsohn, Joel, Margaret E. Bentley, Pertti J. Pelto, Moni Nag, Saroj Pachauri, Abigail D. Harrison, and Laura T. Landman, eds. 1994 *Listening to Women Talk about their Health: Issues and Evidence from India.* New Delhi: Har-Anand Publications.

Glass, Robert H., and Roland J. Ericsson 1982 *Getting Pregnant in the 1980s: New Advances in Infertility Treatment and Sex Preselection.* Berkeley: University of California Press.

Gluck, Sherna B. and Daphne Patai, eds. 1991 *Women's Words: The Feminist Practice of Oral History.* New York: Routledge.

Goodkind, Daniel. 1999 "Should Prenatal Selection be Restricted? Ethical Questions and their Implications for Research and Policy." *Population Studies* 53(1): 49–61.

Gorrie, Trula M., Emily S. McKinney, and Sharon S. Murray 1998 *Foundations of Maternal-Newborn Nursing.*

Philadelphia: W. B. Saunders Company.

Griffiths, Paula, Zoë Mathews, and Andrew Hinde 2000 "Understanding the Sex Ratio in India: A Simulation Approach." *Demography* 37(4): 477–488.

Guilmoto Christopher Z. and Isabelle Attané 2007 "The Geography of Deteriorating Child Sex Ratio in China and India." In *Watering the Neighbor's Garden: The Growing Female Deficit in Asia.* Isabella Attané and Christopher Z. Guilmoto, eds. pp. 109–129. Paris: Committee for International Cooperation and National Research in Demography.

Gupta, Jyotsna Agnihotri 1991 "Women's Bodies: The Site for the Ongoing Conquest by Reproductive Technologies." *Issues in Reproductive and Genetic Engineering* 4(2): 93–107.

Gupta, Jyotsna Agnihotri 2000 *New Reproductive Technologies, Women's Health and Autonomy: Freedom or Dependency?* New Delhi: Sage Publications.

Gwatkin, Davidson, R. 1979 "Political Will and Family Planning: The Implications of India's Emergency Experience." *Population and Development Review* 5(1): 29–59.

Harlan, Lindsey and Paul B. Courtright, eds. 1995 *From the Margins of Hindu Marriage: Essays on Gender, Religion, and Culture.* New York: Oxford University Press.

Hesketh, Therese, Li Lu, and Zhu Wei Xing 2005 "The Effect of China's One-Child Policy after 25 Years." *The New England Journal of Medicine* 353(11): 1171–1176.

Holmes, Helen B. and Betty B. Hoskins 1987 "Prenatal and Preconception Sex Choice Technologies: A Path to Femicide?" In *Man-Made Women: How New Reproductive Technologies Affect Women.* Gena Corea, , Renate Duelli Klein,

Jalna Hanmer, Helen B. Holmes, Betty Hoskins, Madhu Kishwar, Janice Raymond, Robyn Rowland, and Roberta Steinbacher, eds. pp. 15–29. Bloomington: Indiana University Press.

Ibbetson, Denzil 1916 *Punjab Castes.* Lahore: India Press.

Indian Council of Medical Research 1989 *Illegal Abortions in Rural Areas: A Taskforce Study.* Indian Council of Medical Research: New Delhi.

Jeffery, Patricia and Roger Jeffery 1996 *Don't Marry Me to a Plowman! Women's Everyday Lives in Rural North India.* Boulder, CO: Westview Press.

Jeffery, Roger, Patricia Jeffery, and Andrew Lyon 1984 "Female Infanticide and Amniocentesis." *Social Science & Medicine* 19(11): 1207–1212.

Kabra, S.G. 1986 "Terminate Pregnancy, Do not Exterminate Women." *Manushi* 36: 25.

Khanna, Sunil K. 1995 "Prenatal Sex Determination: A New Family-Building Strategy." *Manushi* 86: 23–29.

Khanna, Sunil K. 1997 "Traditions and Reproductive Technology in an Urbanizing North Indian Village." *Social Science & Medicine* 44(2): 171–180.

Khanna, Sunil K. 1999 "*Prenatal Sex Determination and Sex–selective Abortion in India: Some Legal Considerations*." *The Anthropologist* 1(1): 61–71.

Khanna, Sunil K. 2001 "Pahari Jatni: Marriage, Networks, and Gender Ethnicity in an Urbanizing Jat Village in North India." *The Anthropologist* 2(4): 11–19.

Khanna, Sunil K. 2001 "Shahri Jat and Dehati Jatni: The Indian Peasant Community in Transition." *Contemporary South Asia* 10(1): 37–53.

Khanna, Sunil K. 2004 "Jats." In *Encyclopedia of Medical Anthropology: Health and Illness in the World's Cultures (Volume 2: Cultures)*. Carol R.

Embers and Melvin Embers, eds. pp. 777–783. New York: Kluwer Academic/Plenum Publishers.

Kim, Doo-Sub 2004 "Missing Girls in South Korea: Trends, Levels, and Regional Variations." *Population* 59(6): 865–878.

Kishwar, Madhu 1995 "When Daughters are Unwanted: Sex Determination Tests in India." *Manushi* 86: 15–22.

Kumar, Dharma 1983 "Amniocentesis Again." *Economic and Political Weekly* 18: 1075–1076.

Kusum 1993 "The Use of Pre-natal Diagnostic Techniques for Sex Selection: The Indian Scene." *Bioethics* 7(2/3): 149–165.

Lamphere, Louise 2000 "The Public Face of Anthropology." *Anthropology Newsletter* 41(1): 48.

Lavely, William, Jianke Li, and Jianghong Li 2001 "Sex Preference for Children in a Meifu Li Community in Hainan, China." *California Center for Population Research On-Line Working Paper Series*. Las Angeles: University of California.

Lewis, Oscar 1965 *Village Life in Northern India.* Urbana: University of Illinois Press.

Löfstedt, Petra, Luo Shusheng, and Annika Johansson 2004 "Abortion Patterns and Reported Sex Ratios at Birth in Rural Yunnan, China." *Reproductive Health Matters* 12(24): 86–95.

Luthra, Rashmi 1993 "Toward a Reconceptualization of Choice': Challenges by Women at the Margins." *Feminist Issues* 13(1): 41–53.

Luthra, Rashmi 1994 "A Case of Problematic Diffusion: The Use of Sex Determination Techniques in India." *Knowledge: Creation, Diffusion, and Utilization* 15(3): 259–272.

Luthra, Rashmi 1999 "The Women's Movement and the Press in India: The Construction of Female Feticide as a Social Issue." *Women's Studies in Communication* 22(1): 1–24.

Malarkey, Louise M. and Mary E. McMorrow 2000 *Nurse's Manual of Laboratory Tests and Diagnostic Procedures*. Philadelphia: W. B. Saunders Company.

Mandelbaum, David G. 1988 *Women's Seclusion and Men's Honor: Sex Roles in North India, Bangladesh, and Pakistan*. Tucson: The University of Arizona Press.

Mann, Kamlesh 1988 "Status Portrait of Jat Women." *Indian Anthropologist* 18: 51–67.

Miller, Barbara D. 1981 *The Endangered Sex: Neglect of Female Children in Rural North India*. Ithaca: Cornell University Press.

Miller, Barbara D. 1985 "Prenatal and Postnatal Sex Selection in India: The Patriarchal Context, Ethical Questions and Public Policy." *Working Paper #107, Women in International Development Publication Series*. Michigan: Michigan State University.

Miller, Barbara D. 2001 "Female Selective Abortion in Asia: Patterns, Policies, and Debates." *American Anthropologist* 103(4): 1083–1095.

Mines, Diane P. and Sarah Lamb, eds. 2002 *Everyday Life in South Asia*. Bloomington: Indiana University Press.

Ministry of Women and Child Development 2007 *National Report on "A World Fit for Children."* New Delhi: Government of India.

Minturn, Leigh 1993 *Sita's Daughters: Coming out of Purdah*. New York: Oxford University Press.

Moen, Elizabeth 1991 "Sex-Selective Eugenic Abortion: Prospects in China and India." *Issues in Reproductive and Genetic Engineering* 4(3): 231–249.

Oomman, Nandani and Bela R. Ganatra 2002 "Sex Selection: The Systematic

Elimination of Girls." *Reproductive Health Matters* 10(19): 184–188.

Pachauri, Saroj 1994 "Women's Reproductive Health in India: Research Needs and Priorities." In *Listening to Women Talk about their Health: Issues and Evidence from India*. Gittelsohn, Joel, Margaret E. Bentley, Pertti, J. Pelto, Moni Nag, Saroj Pachauri, Abigail D. Harrison, and Laura T. Landman, eds. pp. 15–39, New Delhi: Har-Anand Publications.

Pachauri, Saroj 1997 "Defining a Reproductive Health Package for India: A Proposed Framework." In *Gender Population and Development*. Maithreyi Krishnaraj, Ratna M. Sudarshan, and Abusaleh Shariff, eds. pp. 310–339. New Delhi: Oxford University Press.

Pachauri, Saroj 1998 "Unmet Reproductive and Sexual Health Needs in South Asia." *Journal of Health and Population in Developing Countries* 1(2): 29–30.

Pakrasi, Kanti B. 1970 *Female Infanticide in India*. Calcutta: Editions India.

Pakrasi, Kanti B. and Ajit Haldar 1971 "Sex Ratios and Sex Consequences of Birth in India." *Journal of Biosocial Research* 3: 377–387.

Parikh, Manju 1990 "Sex-Selective Abortion in India: Parental Choice or Sexist Discrimination." *Feminist Issues* 10(2): 19–32.

Patel, Tulsi, ed. 2007 *Sex-Selective Abortion in India: Gender, Society, and New Reproductive Technologies*. New Delhi: Sage Publications.

Patel, Vibhuti 1989 "Sex-Determination and Sex-Preselection Tests in India: Modern Techniques of Femicide." *Bulletin of Concerned Asian Scholars* 21(1): 2–11.

Patel, Vibhuti 2003 "Declining Sex Ratio and New Reproductive Technologies." *Health Action* 16(7-8): 30–33.

Patel, Vibhuti 2007 "The Political Economy of Missing Girls in India." In *Sex-Selective Abortions in India: Gender, Society, and New Reproductive Technologies*. Tulsi Patel, ed. pp. 286–315. New Delhi: Sage Publications.

Pradhan, Mahesh Chandra 1966 *The Political System of the Jats of Northern India*. Bombay: Oxford University Press.

Qanungo, Kalika-Ranjan 1925 *History of the Jats: Contribution to the History of Northern India*. New Delhi: Surajmal Memorial Education Society (reprinted in 1982).

Ramanamma, A. and U. Bambawale 1980 "The Mania for Sons: An Analysis of Social Values in South Asia." *Social Science & Medicine 14B:* 107–110.

Rao, Mohan, ed. 2004 *The Unheard Scream: Reproductive Health and Women's Lives in India*. Zubaan: New Delhi.

Report of the Joint Committee 1992 *The Prenatal Diagnostic Techniques (Regulation and Prevention of Misuse) Bill, 1991*. New Delhi: Lok Sabha Secretariat.

Riley, Nancy E. 2004 "China's Population: New Trends and Challenges." *Population Bulletin* 59(2). Washington, DC: Population Reference Bureau.

Roberts, Elizabeth 2006 "God's Laboratory: Religious Rationalities and Modernity in Ecuadorian In-Vitro Fertilization." *Culture, Medicine and Psychiatry* 30(4): 507–536.

Rutherford, Robert and T. K. Roy 2003 "Factors Affecting Sex-Selective Abortion in India and 17 Major States." *National Family Health Survey Subject Report 21*. Honolulu: East-West Center.

Sabharwal, Yogesh Kumar 2006. "Eradication of Female Feticide." Lecture delivered on December 17, 2006, in Patiala, Punjab.

Sagar, Alpana D. 2007 "Between a Rock and a Hard Place: The Social Context of the Missing Girl Child." In *Sex-Selective Abortions in India: Gender, Society, and New Reproductive Technologies*. Tulsi Patel, ed. pp. 175–202. New Delhi: Sage Publications.

Santhya, K. G. 2003 "Changing Family Planning Scenario in India: An Overview of Recent Evidence." *Regional Working Paper, South and East Asia*. Population Council, New Delhi, India.

Sen, Amartya 1990 "More Than 100 Million Women are Missing." *The New York Review of Books* 37(20).

Sen, Amartya 2003 "Missing Women–Revisited." *British Medical Journal* 327: 1297–1298.

Sharma, S. 2006 "Feticides Shoot Past Alarm Bell." *The Hindustan Times* (March 6th).

Shiva, Mira, Roma Solomon, and Manila Jose, eds. 1995 *Proceedings of the Workshop at Voluntary Health Association of India*. New Delhi: Voluntary Health Association of India.

Shore, Chris 1992 "Virgin Births and Sterile Debates: Anthropology and the New Reproductive Technologies." *Current Anthropology* 33(3): 295–314.

Shukla, S., Sanjeev Kulkarni, and Vibhuti Patel 1987 "Abuse of New Technology." *Seminar* 331: 14–17.

Shurmer-Smith, Pamela 2000 *India: Globalization and Change*. New York: Oxford University Press.

Shuzhua Li, Wei Yan, Jiang Quanbao, and Macrus W. Feldman 2007 "Imbalanced Sex Ratio at Birth and Female Child Survival in China: Issues and Prospects." In *Watering the Neighbor's Garden: The Growing Female Deficit in Asia*. Isabella Attané and Christopher Z. Guilmoto, eds. pp. 25–47. Paris: Committee for International Cooperation and National Research in Demography.

Singer, Milton 1972 *When a Great Tradition Modernizes: An Anthropological Approach to Indian Civilization.* Chicago: University of Chicago Press.

Srinivas, Mysore N. 1976 *The Village Remembered.* Berkeley: University of California Press.

Srinivas, Mysore N. and E. A. Ramaswamy 1977 *Culture and Human Fertility in India.* Delhi: Oxford University Press.

Stanworth, Michelle, ed. 1987 *Reproductive Technologies: Gender, Motherhood, and Medicine.* Minneapolis: University of Minnesota Press.

Steinbacher, R. and G. Faith 1990 "Sex Selection Technology: A Prediction for its Use and Effect." *Journal of Psychology: Interdisciplinary and Applied* 124(3): 283–288.

Strathern, Marilyn 1992 *Reproducing the Future: Essays on Anthropology, Kinship, and the New Reproductive Technologies.* Manchester: Manchester University Press.

Strathern, Marilyn 1995 "Displacing Knowledge: Technology and the Consequences for Kinship." In *Conceiving the New World Order: The Global Politics of Reproduction.* Faye D. Ginsburg and Rayna Rapp, eds. pp. 346–363. Berkeley: University of California Press.

Sudha, Shreeniwas and S. Irudaya Rajan 1999 "Female Demographic Disadvantage in India 1981–1991: Sex-Selective Abortion and Female Infanticide." *Development and Change: Special Issue of Gender, Poverty, and Well-Being* 30: 585–618.

Tanne, Janice Hopkins 2005 "Home Test Shows Sex of Fetus at Five Weeks of Pregnancy." *British Medical Journal* 331 (7508): 69.

The Hindustan *Times* 1999 "Jats Included in the List of Other Backward Communities (OBC)" (October 18th).

Times of India 1982 "Editorial on Amniocentesis." *New Delhi* (June 1982).

Times of India 2008 "[India] Government to Review Implementation of PCPNDT (Sex-Selection Act)" (July 14th).

Unisa, Sayeed, C. P. Prakasam, R. K. Sinha, and R. B. Bhagat 2003 *Evidence of Sex Selective Abortion from Two Cultural Settings of India: A Study of Haryana and Tamil Nadu.* Mumbai: International Institute for Population Sciences.

United Nations Children's Fund 2007 *The State of World's Children 2007. Women and Children: Double Dividend of Gender Equity.* New York: UNICEF.

United State Census 2005 *International Database (IDB).* Washington, D.C.: US Census Bureau.

Unnikrishnan, P. V. 1993 "Banned – Select: A Drug to Alter the Sex of the Fetus." *Health for the Millions* 1(2): 29–30.

Vallianatos, Helen 2006 *Poor and Pregnant in New Delhi, India.* Edmonton, Alberta: Qual Institute Press.

Voluntary Health Association of India 1993 *Women and Health: Issues Relating to Sex Determination Testing.* New Delhi: Voluntary Health Association of India.

Wadley, Susan S. 1993 "Family Composition Strategies in Rural North India." *Social Science & Medicine* 37: 1367–1376.

Wadley, Susan S. 1994 *Struggling with Destiny in Karimpur, 1925–1984.* Berkeley: University of California Press.

Wertz, Dorothy C. and John C. Fletcher 1989 "Fatal knowledge? Prenatal Diagnosis and Sex Selection." *The Hastings Center Report* 19(3): 21–27.

Westphal-Hellbusch, Sigrid and H. Westphal 1964 *The Jat of Pakistan.* Berlin: Duncker & Humbolt.

Whitlow, B. J., M. S. Lazanakis, and D. L. Economides 1999 "The Sonographic Identification of Fetal Gender from 11 to 14 Weeks of Gestation."

Ultrasound in Obstetrics and Gynecology 13(5): 301–304.

Williamson, Nancy E. 1976 *Sons or Daughters: A Cross-Cultural Survey of Parental Preferences*. California: Sage Publications.

Wonacott, Peter 2007 "India's Skewed Sex Ratio puts GE Sales in Spotlight." *The Wall Street Journal* (April 19th).

Yan, Yunxiang 2003 *Private Life under Socialism: Love, Intimacy, and Family Change in a Chinese Village, 1949–1999*. Stanford: Stanford University Press.

Zuanna, Dalla G. and Tiziana Leone 2001 "A Gender Preference Measure: The Sex Ratio at Last Birth." *Genus LVII(1–2)*: 1–12.

Index